Sophia

The Wisdom of God

ESALEN INSTITUTE / LINDISFARNE PRESS
LIBRARY OF RUSSIAN PHILOSOPHY

In the same series:

Sophia

The Wisdom of God

An Outline of Sophiology

Sergei Bulgakov

LINDISFARNE PRESS

This book is a revised edition of *The Wisdom of God: A Brief Summary of Sophiology*, translated from the Russian by the Rev. Patrick Thompson, the Rev. O. Fielding Clarke and Miss Xenia Braikevitc, published by The Paisley Press, Inc., New York, N.Y. and Williams and Norgate, Ltd., London, 1937.

Published by Lindisfarne Press
RR 4, Box 94 A-1, Hudson, N.Y. 12534

Library of Congress Cataloging-in-Publication Data

Bulgakov, Sergei Nikolaevich, 1871–1944.
  Sophia, the wisdom of God : an outline of sophiology / Sergei Bulgakov.
    p. cm—(Library of Russian philosophy)
  Translated from an unpublished Russian manuscript.
  Rev. ed. of: The Wisdom of God. 1937.
  Includes bibliographical references and index.
  ISBN 0-940262-60-6
  1. God—Wisdom. 2. Wisdom (Biblical personification)—History of
doctrines. 3. Wisdom—Religious aspects—Orthodox Eastern Church.
4. Russkaia pravoslavnaia tserkov—Doctrines. 5. Orthodox Eastern
 Church—Doctrines.   I. Bulgakov, Sergei Nikolaevich, 1871–1944.
Wisdom of God.   II. Title.   III. Series.
BT150.B8   1993   93–5691
231' .6—dc20

10 9 8 7 6 5 4 3 2 1

Printed in the United States of America

CONTENTS

FOREWORD

Let it be known: today the Eternal Feminine
In an incorruptible body is descending to Earth.
In the unfading light of the new goddess
Heaven has become one with the deeps.

Vladimir Solovyov

Where the Spirit of the Lord is, there is freedom.

2 Corinthians. 3:17

It is true, as Caitlin Matthews writes, that "Sophia has always been at home in Russia"—the motherland—where in the soul of the people "Moist Mother Earth" has always been venerated, and at times even identified, as the Mother of God and the dwelling of the Holy Spirit. Enthroned in icons and images, the center of deep popular devotion, Sophia always lived a dreamlife in the Russian heart. But it was not until the last century that she awoke into philosophy, entering and illuminating the light of consciousness itself.

First, Vladimir Solovyov was granted three prophetic visions of Sophia (one in 1862, two in 1875). On the basis of the passionate, personal relationship epitomized by these encounters, enriched as these were by close study of other witnesses to Sophia's approach (such as Paracelsus, Boehme, Gichtel, John Pordage, Jane Leade, Gottfried Arnold, Emmanuel Swedenborg, and Franz von Baader), as well as early Gnostics, such as Valentinus, Solovyov was able to forge a new philosophical and cosmological understanding of the Divine Feminine. What Solovyov began was continued by poets like Alexander Blok and Andrei Beli, and theologian-philosophers like the Princes S. N. and E. N. Trubetskoy. Then with the publication in 1913 of Pavel Florensky's *The Pillar and Foundation of the Truth*, Sophia—"the Great Root of the whole creation"—began her journey into Christian theology, a journey that Sergei Bulgakov brought closer to its destination.

Sergei Nikolaievich Bulgakov was born in 1871 in Central Russia, in Livny, in the province of Oryol, where his father was a priest. "I grew up near the parish of St. Sergius," he writes, "in the gracious atmosphere of its prayers and within the sound of its bells. The aesthetic, moral, and everyday recollections of my childhood are bound up with the life of that parish church." Like so many others, Bulgakov's path to Christianity was not straightforward, but had to pass through the crucible of modern thought. In early adolescence, while in seminary, he experienced a religious crisis. This was "painful but not tragic." Losing his faith, he adopted the revolutionary spirit of the intelligentsia: he became a Marxist. In this mood, he attended Moscow University, where he studied law.

In 1896, he published his first work: *The Role of the Market in Capitalist Production*. In the same year, the process of his conversion began:

> I was twenty-four years old. For a decade I had lived without faith and, after stormy doubts, a religious emptiness reigned in my soul. One evening, we were driving across the southern steppes of Russia.

The strong scented spring grass was gilded by the rays of a glorious sunset. Far in the distance, I saw the blue outlines of the Caucasus. This was my first sight of the mountains. I gazed with ecstatic delight at their rising slopes. I drank in the light and air of the steppes. I listened to the revelation of nature. My soul was used to the dull pain of seeing nature as a lifeless desert and of treating its surface beauty as a deceptive mask. Yet, contrary to my intellectual convictions, I could not be reconciled to nature without God.

Suddenly and joyfully in that evening hour my soul was stirred. I started to wonder what would happen if the cosmos were not a desert and its beauty not a mask or deception—if nature were not death, but life. What if the merciful and loving Father existed, if nature was a vestige of his love and glory, and if the pious feelings of my childhood, when I used to live in his presence, when I loved him and trembled because I was weak—what if all this were true. . . .

O mountains of the Caucasus! I saw your ice sparkling from sea to sea, your snows reddening under the morning dawn, the peaks which pierced the sky, and my soul melted in ecstasy. . . . The first day of creation shone before my eyes. Everything was clear, everything was at peace and full of ringing joy. My heart was ready to break with bliss. There is no life and no death, only one eternal and unmovable now. *Nunc dimittis* rang out in my heart and in nature. And an unexpected feeling rose up and grew within me—the sense of victory over death. At that moment

I wanted to die, my soul felt a sweet longing for death in order to melt away joyfully, ecstatically, into that which towered up, sparkled and shone with the beauty of first creation. . . . And that moment of meeting did not die in my soul, that apocalypse, that wedding feast: the first encounter with Sophia. That of which the mountains spoke to me in their solemn brilliance, I soon recognized again in the shy, gentle, girlish look on different shores and under different mountains. . . . (*The Unfading Light*)

Graduating from Moscow University and still under the spell of Marxism—"which suited me about as much as a saddle fits a cow"—Bulgakov spent the years 1898-1900 in Germany. He expected much from the land of Marx and social democracy. His admiration for Western culture was boundless. Yet, contrary to all his expectations, he was disappointed. His apparently firm convictions began to dissolve a second time. Once again, an unexpected, miraculous encounter occurred—this time in Dresden, with Raphael's *Sistine Madonna*:

It was a foggy autumn morning. I went to the art gallery to do my duty as a tourist. My knowledge of European painting was negligible. I did not know what to expect. The eyes of the Heavenly Queen, the Mother who holds in her arms the Eternal Infant, pierced my soul. There was in them an immense power of purity and of prophetic self-sacrifice—the knowledge of suffering and the readiness for free suffering, and the same prophetic readiness for sacrifice that was to be seen in the unchildishly wise eyes of the Child.... I cried joyful, yet bitter tears, and with them the ice melted from my soul, and some of my psychological knots were loosened. This was an aesthetic emotion, but it was also a new knowledge; it was a miracle. I was still a Marxist, but I was obliged to call my contemplation of the Madonna by the name of "prayer." ...

(The Unfading Light)

In 1901, back from Germany, Bulgakov became a lecturer in Political Economy at the Kiev Polytechnic Institute. By this time, he was moving toward a recovery of faith. Already in his second book, *Capitalism and Agriculture* (1900), he had realized that the Marxist law of the concentrations of production could not apply to agriculture, which was, by nature, decentralized. But before he could discover the full incarnationism appropriate to the full recognition of the absoluteness of Christ's sacrifice, Bulgakov had to pass through the philosophical consciousness inaugurated by German idealism (Kant and Hegel). This move, requiring a reconciliation, if not a union, of philosophical and religious experience, opened him to new, epistemological paths to transformation. These allied him both with the more gnostic, Sophiological impulse of Vladimir Solovyov and with the more orthodox, religious striving of Pavel Florensky. At the same time, inner destiny led him to becoming a leader—with Nikolai Berdyaev, Piotr Struve, Valdimir Ern and others—of the turn-of-the-century Russian "religious renaissance." As part of this Bulgakov published, in 1904, *From Marxism to Idealism,* and began to edit (with Berdyaev) a series of journals: first, *Novy Put* ("The New Way") and then *Voprosy Zhisni* ("The Problems of Life"), which he founded with Berdyaev. At this point (1906), Bulgakov returned from Kiev to Moscow to teach at the Commercial Institute. Now more than halfway to full, living knowledge of God, Bulgakov was still prey to doubt and hesitation. It would take another encounter to complete his transformation. This occurred in 1908:

> It was autumn, a sunny day and a familiar northern landscape. I made my way to a solitary hermitage lost in the forest. I was still in the clutches of confusion and impotence. I had come with a friend—secretly I hoped I would meet God. But my determination deserted me completely. At vespers I remained cold and unfeeling. When the prayer for those preparing for confession began, I almost ran out of the Church. I left, weeping bitterly. I walked, full of anguish toward the guest, seeing nothing around me. Then suddenly I found myself before the Elder's cell. I had been led there. I had intended to go in another direction, but absent-mindedly took the wrong turn. . . . A miracle had happened to me. The Elder, seeing the prodigal son approach, ran to meet me. From him I learned that all human sins were like a drop in the ocean of God's mercy. I left him forgiven and reconciled, trembling and in tears, feeling as if I were carried on wings. . . .
>
> (*The Unfading Light*)

From this moment on, Sergei Bulgakov moved unerringly toward Orthodoxy, becoming a priest in 1918. After the Revolution, he fled to the Crimea, where he wrote and lectured until 1922, when he was expelled from Russia. As a refugee, he landed first at Constantinople, where he experienced firsthand the source of Russian Christianity, the Cathedral of Holy Wisdom, *Hagia Sophia*. It was here, a millennium before, that Vladimir's emissaries had witnessed the *beauty* that they felt was the sign of true religion. For, according to "The Primary Chronicle," being urged by all sides to convert to their religion—by the Bulgarians to convert to Islam, by the Germans to Roman Christianity, by the Jews to Judaism, and by the Greeks to their religion—Vladimir determined to send emissaries to discover the fine points of each. This they did, reporting:

> When we journeyed among the Bulgarians, we beheld how they worship in their temple, called a mosque, while they stand ungirt. The Bulgarian bows, sits down, looks hither and thither like one possessed, and there is no happiness among them. . . . Their religion is not good. Then we went among the Germans, and saw them performing many ceremonies; but we beheld no glory there. Then we went on to Greece, and the Greeks led us to the edifices where they worship their God, and we knew not whether we were in heaven or on earth. For on earth there is no such splendor or such beauty, and we are at a loss to know how to describe it. We only know that God dwells there among men, and their service is fairer than the ceremonies of other nations.

Bulgakov's experience echoed that of these first witnesses. His happiness was boundless. God had not let him die without a vision of St. Sophia as "something absolute, self-evident, and irrefutable." It was the most marvellous of churches—human tongue could not express its lightness, clarity, inner transparency, and wonderful harmony:

> This is indeed Sophia, the real unity of the world in the Logos, the co-inherence of all with all, the world of divine ideas. . . . The pagan Sophia of Plato beholds herself mirrored in the Christian Sophia, the divine Wisdom. Truly, the temple of St. Sophia is the artistic, tangible proof and manifestation of St. Sophia—of the Sophianic nature of the world and the cosmic nature of Sophia. It is neither heaven nor earth, but the vault of heaven above the earth. We perceive here neither God nor man, but divinity, the divine veil thrown over the world. How true was our ancestors' feeling in this temple, how right they were in saying they did not know whether they were in heaven or on earth! Indeed, they were neither in heaven nor on earth, they were in St. Sophia— between the two. . . . (*Autobiographical Notes*)

After Constantinople, Bulgakov went first to Prague, where he worked closely with Piotr Struve and others, and helped organize the Russian Church in exile. Then, in 1925, he was appointed Professor and Dean at the newly established Russian Theological Institute in Paris.

In Paris he began his major theological work. This took the form of two ambitious "trilogies." The first concerned the three figures surrounding Christ in the Russian "deeisis" —Mary, the Mother of God (*The Burning*

Bush, 1927); St. John the Baptist (*The Friend of the Bride-groom*, 1927); and the Angels (*Jacob's Ladder*, 1929.) The second dealt with the reality of the divinization of humanity and the cosmos through the deed of Christ: "Divine Humanity." These three profound works (*The Lamb of God*, 1933; *The Comforter*, 1936; and the posthumously published *The Bride of the Lamb*, 1945) articulated Bulgakov's mature understanding of Sophia. At the same time, he was active in the Ecumenical Movement, taking part in the Lausanne (1926), Oxford (1937), and Edinburgh (1937) conferences. He also travelled frequently to England, where he contributed to the work of the Fellowship of St. Alban and St. Sergius—which explains why the present work first appeared in English.

In 1939, Father Bulgakov lost his voice, following an operation for cancer of the throat. Yet he continued to teach and lecture—above all, giving his lectures on *The Apocalypse of John* (first published posthumously in 1948.) Learning to speak "without a voice," he continued to celebrate the early morning Liturgy—until Whit Monday, 1944. That morning he celebrated the Liturgy as usual. But that night he was found unconscious. He died forty days later, on July 12, 1944.

. . . . .

Two intuitions—twin items of faith—continuously guided and comforted Sergei Bulgakov on his journey: the reality of the primacy and ubiquity of revelation and the fact of the interdependence and interconnection of all things. Everything is a revelation of God and thus bears God's stamp everywhere. That is to say that for all creatures whose hearts (and eyes and ears) are opened the nearness of Creator—his speech and wisdom—is self-evident. By this token, too, all is interconnected. Theology, philosophy, science, art are not separate disciplines, but parts of one and the same wisdom, of the same apprehension of Sophia, manifested to us in creation and in the Scriptures, in nature and in the Church. In the words of Lev Zander, "true love of wisdom, true philo-Sophia must take everything into account: it cannot be based upon any particular set of facts, but has to reckon with the fullness of God's revelation in the world."

Bulgakov's path to true philo-Sophia passed through two movements. The first, beginning with *The Unfading Light* (1917), written before he took holy orders, develops the idea of the cosmic Sophia as the intelligible basis of the world—the soul of the world, the wisdom of nature. Three ideas guided his explorations: the nature of "religious consciousness," in which a human being strives for knowledge of God and God answers this striving with revelation; and behind this, the mystical experience, "Thou seest me always," the implication of which is that the light of consciousness proceeds from God and leads to God. But how, with such an intuition, to avoid the errors of pantheism and sheer immanentism? An *intermediary* is needed, a boundary between the Nothing of the Creator and the multiplicity of the cosmos. This boundary between the Creator and creation, between God and the world, is Sophia. Sophia is the divine "Idea," the object of God's love: "the love of love" (Lossky). "Sophia is loved and loves in return, and through this reciprocal love she receives all, is all." By giving herself wholly up to God she receives all from God. Receiving her essence from the Father, she is the creature and daughter of God; knowing and known by the Word, she is the bride of the Son and the spouse of the Lamb; receiving the gifts of the Spirit, she is the Church and, at the same time, Mary; and she is the ideal soul of creation—the world soul, *natura naturans*— *Beauty*. As Dostoievsky wrote: "Beauty will save the world." In Bulgakov, this Sophianic beauty manifests through the life-giving power of the Spirit, who is never apart from the Word or meaning.

Therefore Sophia is twofold, at once Divine and creaturely—above and before creation *and* "in" creation. The world is created in Sophia and Sophia, at the same time, is in the world, throughout it, in the form of divine energies and spiritual beings, as its boundary. Hence creation is, as it were, "the separation of Sophia's potentiality from her actuality." In the world, Sophia is *actualized*—as the earth's eros for heaven, all creation "longing for liberation from the bondage of corruption, for the radiance of Sophianic light, for beauty and transfiguration."

At the same time Sophia, as divine *Life*, is at once the "panorganism" or organic totality of Ideas in God and the archetype of eternal humanity in God—the very basis of the being of the human soul. As Pavel Florensky had written:

This Great Being, both royal and feminine, who being neither God nor the Eternal Son of God, neither angel nor saint, receives the veneration of the One who accomplishes the Old Testament, as well as of the One who is the begetter of the New Testament: who is she, then, but the truest humanity, the purest and most whole of beings, the macrocosmic whole, the living soul of nature and of the universe eternally united and uniting in the process of time with the Divine and uniting with all that is.

(The Pillar and Foundation of the Truth)

One Sophia—or Cosmic Humanity—is thus both in God and in creation. "The Divine Sophia became the created Sophia"—this is the meaning of creation and human beings. Therefore "every creature must be recognized as sophianic insofar as its positive content or its idea, which is its basis or norm, is concerned; but it should not be forgotten that creatures have another aspect—the lower 'substratum' of the world, matter as 'nothing' raised into being and striving to embody the Sophian principle in itself."

The healing value of Sophia for our time is manifold. Besides the obvious one of restoring (in principle, at least) the feminine element to creation and the divine, two related aspects stand out as worthy of particular mention. In the first place, meditation on Sophia (along the lines suggested by Bulgakov) begins the process of the resacralization of nature and the cosmos—of reconnecting humanity to God by the intermediary of creation viewed as a *theophany* or divine manifestation. This aspect, by providing a metaphysical or theological foundation, can transform the profane science of ecology into an *ecosophy* which unites aesthetic, moral, and natural scientific approaches to nature. Second, Sophia, whose "other" name is Love, is inevitably concrete and can be known only in embodied human actions. That is to say, the knowledge of Sophia in nature can only be realized by human beings whose social and relational life is a living expression "in deed and in truth" of that love of which St. John speaks in his Epistle when he writes, "Beloved, let us love one another: for love is of God; and everyone that loveth is born of God and knoweth God. He that loveth not knoweth not God; for God is love. . . ; and he that dwelleth in love dwelleth in God, and God in him. . . . We love him because he first loved us."

. . . . .

In his later, less philosophical works, Father Bulgakov sought to place his understanding of Sophia on a more strictly theological basis and to interpret the foundations of Christian dogma of the Incarnation and the Trinity in the light of Sophiology. *Sophia, the Wisdom of God* belongs to this period. By this time, however, Bulgakov had already raised the ire of more conservative theologians, who suspected him of heresy. Already in 1927 the Holy Synod of the Russian Emigré Church had accused the Russian Theological Seminary in Paris of "modernism" and "freemasonry." The bone of contention was Sophia:

> Until now, in accord with the Apostle Paul and the Church Fathers, we have recognized only "Christ crucified, unto the Jews a stumbling block, and unto the Greeks foolishness. . . . Christ, the power of God, and the wisdom of God." But now they to the contrary enunciate a new doctrine of "Sophia, the feminine principle in God." At times, for them, this feminine principle is an individual substance, a hypostasis who while not being consubstantial with the Holy Trinity is at the same time removed from it. At times this feminine principle appears to them

only as a "hypostatic" mode analogous to the hypostasis. In the first case Wisdom is a being superior to the Mother of God and worthy of cult and adoration, in the second case she is practically identified with the Holy Virgin. They themselves do not provide an exact account of their doctrine. But whatever it might be, both interpretations of "Sophia" are absolutely foreign to the tradition of the Apostles and the Patristic teachings.

· · · · ·

The controversy climaxed in 1935-37. Bulgakov was accused of condescension toward Church tradition, intellectualism, gnosticism, an overactive imagination—and even of creating a fourth hypostasis or at least of infusing masculine and feminine elements into the members of the Trinity. He was censured. The Moscow Patriarchy recommended that he be deprived of all teaching and priestly duties. Wearily, Bulgakov defended himself. At the same time, works were published in his defense. *Sophia, the Wisdom of God*, though by no means an apologetic work, arises in this context. It is the clearest statement of his mature position and an invaluable guide to all who seek a *theological* understanding of Sophia.

CHRISTOPHER BAMFORD

A Bibliography of Works by Sergei Bulgakov

The following are Bulgakov's main works.
All are in Russian, except where indicated.

1896 *The Role of the Market in Capitalist Production* (Moscow)

1901 *Capitalism and Agriculture* (Moscow)

1903 *From Marxism to Idealism.* Collected Articles (1896-1903, St. Petersburg)

1911 *Two Cities. Inquiries on the nature of Social Idealism.* Vol. I-II (Moscow)

1912 *The Philosophy of Economics, Part I: The World as Economics* (Moscow)

1917 *The Unfading Light. Intuitions and Speculations* (Moscow)

1918 *Quiet Thoughts. Collected Articles* (1911-1915) (Moscow)

1925 *Person and Personality. Scholia to The Unfading Light.* (Symposium in Honor of P.B. Struve) (Prague)

1926 *St. Peter and St. John* (Paris); *The Legacy of St. Sergius to Russian Theology.* "Puit" No. 5 (Paris)

1927 *The Burning Bush* (On the Orthodox Cult of the Virgin) (Paris); *The Friend of the Bridegroom* (On the Orthodox Veneration of John the Baptist) (Paris); *The Tragedy of Philosophy* (Darmstadt: in German)

1928 (and 1930) *Chapters on the Trinity.* "Orthodox Thought" No.1 and No.2 (Paris)

1929 *Karl Marx as a Religious Type; Jacob's Ladder* (On Angels) (Warsaw and Paris)

1930 *The Eucharistic Dogma.* "Puit" No.s 20 and 21. Paris; *The Name of God.* A theological inquiry into the philosophy of the word. (Only the first chapter of this work is published in German: *Was ist das Wort in Festschrift*, Th. G. Masaryk.)

1931 *Icons and Their Veneration* (Paris)

1932 *On Miracles in the Gospel* (Paris); *The Holy Grail* (An essay on a dogmatic exegesis of John xix, 34) "Puit," No. 32 (Paris)

1933 *The Lamb of God (Agnus Dei). On God-humanhood* [or *God-manhood*]. *Part I* (Paris: also translated into French); *The Spirit of Dogma.* (After Seven Oecumenical Councils. Speech at the Convocation of the Orthodox Seminary) "Puit," No. 37 (Paris)

1935 *The Orthodox Church* (London: in English); *On Sophia the Wisdom of God.* Ukaze of the Moscow Patriarchate, and reports of Rev. Prof. Sergius Bulgakov to the Metropolitan Eulogius (Paris) (In German: "Orient und Occident," Heft 1, Neue Folge.)

1936 *The Comforter. On God-humanhood* [or *God-manhood*]. *Part II* (Paris: also translated in French); *More on the Problem of Sophia, the Wisdom of God.* (With reference to the decision of the Bishop's Council in Karlovtsi. Also in "Puit," No. 50 (Paris); *Zur Frage nach der Weisheit Gottes.* Thesem zum Vortrag ueber die Sophiologie, vorgelegt auf der Englis-chen-russischen Theologienconferenz in Mirfield am 28 April (Keftz)

1937 (Sophia) *The Wisdom of God* (London: in English); *From Marxism to Sophiology* (Lecture, in English) *The Review of Religion*, Vol. 1. No.4 (New York)

1945 *The Bride of the Lamb* (Paris)

1946 *Autobiographical Notes* (Paris)

1948 *The Apocalypse of John* (Paris)

1953 *The Philosophy of the Name* (Paris)

1955 *Life from the Tomb* (Paris)

1959 *The Vatican Dogma* (South Canaan, Pa., in English)

1961 *Dialog between God and Man* (Marbourg)

1965 *Orthodoxy* (Paris)

1973 *Spiritual Journey* (Paris)

Secondary Sources and Background Reading

Cioran, S. *Vladimir Solov'iev and the Knighthood of Divine Sophia.* Waterloo, Ontario: Wilfred Laurier University Press, 1977.

Graves, Charles. *The Holy Spirit in the Theology of Sergius Bulgakov.* Geneva: Privately printed at the World Council of Churches, 1972.

Lossky, N. O. *History of Russian Philosophy.* New York: International Universities Press, 1951.

Matthews, Caitlin. *Sophia, Goddess of Wisdom.* London: Mandala (HarperCollins), 1991.

Pain, J. and Zernov, N. (eds.) *A Bulgakov Anthology.* Philadelphia: The Westminster Press, 1976.

INTRODUCTION

Those who have visited the church of St. Sophia in Constantinople and have fallen under the spell of what it reveals, will find themselves permanently enriched by a new apprehension of the world in God, that is, of the divine Sophia. This heavenly dome, which portrays heaven bending to embrace the earth, gives expression in finite form to the infinite, to an all-embracing unity, to the stillness of eternity, in the form of a work of art which, though belonging to this world, is a miracle of harmony itself. The grace, lightness, simplicity, and wonderful symmetry of the structure account for the fact that the weight of the dome and even of the very walls seems to dissolve completely. An ocean of light pours in from above and dominates the whole space below—it enchants, convinces, as it seems to say: I am in the world and the world is in me. Here Plato is baptized into Christianity, for here, surely, we have the lofty realm to which souls ascend for the contemplation of ideas.

But as Plato's pagan *Sophia* gazes upon herself she learns to recognize herself in the divine *Sophia* and, indeed, this church is an artistic proof of her existence and of her reality, spread like a protecting canopy over the world. It represents the last, silent revelation of the Greek genius, bequeathed to the ages, concerning *Sophia*, the Wisdom of God. Yet this marvel of architecture, though designed in a theological age in obedience to the will of the emperor-theologian, remains without any obvious relationship to the theology of Justinian's epoch. It is a torch kindled for the benefit of subsequent ages. The dome of St. Sophia crowns and as it were summarizes all the theological creativity of the epoch of the Ecumenical Councils. What is the inner meaning of this church of St. Sophia, the Wisdom of God, which is like the swan song of the universal Church in the city of the new Rome? Is it merely a chiselled allegory, such as the churches dedicated to Peace, or Faith, or Hope? The building of this church is a definite landmark in the creative activity of the epoch. For from that time churches dedicated to Sophia began to be built both in Byzantium and in Slavonic countries, with a wealth of mysterious and elusive symbolism. Undoubtedly they are churches dedicated to Christ, but to Christ in the aspect of *Sophia*—to Christ-*Sophia*. What then does this imply? Byzantine theology as such has left behind no explanation of that to which this ecclesiastical architecture bears witness. It only bequeathed its hieroglyphic sophiology, as a theological problem, to the generations which succeeded it.

Nor was this theological problem taken into account or understood by old Rome, the *civitas Dei* as once the *civitas Romana*. There the universality of the Church was looked upon as a kind of spiritual citadel, the *imperium Romanum*, an organization of ecclesiastical authority culminating in the person of the Roman pontiff. The heavenly dome of St. Sophia, which has been suspended as it were in midair, here came to rest on a hierarchical foundation. The dome was no longer the symbol of eternity but of finite limitation. Everything was now defined, determined, coordinated, and correlated under the supreme authority of Christ's representative on earth. Thus in the West the message of Sophia's preeminence enshrined in the churches of St. Sophia was narrowed. In the East, on the other hand, such obstacles never existed. When the faith of Christ was first blazed abroad by the missionaries of Byzantium, there came to the northern land of the Russian tzardom (the "Third Rome"), together with Christianity, this mysterious and as yet undisclosed revelation of *Sophia* enshrined in the hieroglyphics of ecclesiastical architecture.

The first capital of Russia, Kiev, "the mother of Russian towns," was the first to adorn itself, in the eleventh century, with a cathedral of St. Sophia. After this a growing number of churches was so dedicated as the Russian Church, and the influence of the state and of culture in general spread to the North. Moscow, the free city of Nijni-Novgorod, Yaroslavl, and other towns began to build their own churches dedicated to Sophia, the Wisdom of God. Here, too, as in the past, the theological implications of this symbol remained long hidden as a sacred mystery, though they are partially disclosed at this time. It is true that this does not apply to theology, which in the backward conditions of the nation at this period was practically nonexistent, but only to the further

development of sacred symbolism. The sophianic symbol
was first disclosed to some extent in the establishment of
the day of the feast of title. These festivals are associated
with a different range of ideas from those of Byzantium.
The churches of St. Sophia in Russia, as a general rule,
have their feasts of title on feasts of our Lady (in Kiev, the
day of her Nativity; in Novgorod and other places on the
day of her Assumption). Secondly the texts of special ser-
vices to Sophia, though not, it is true, very numerous,
are highly significant. In this way we see that in the interpretation of Sophia, along with the christological emphasis—which corresponds to the *divine* Sophia— another,
mariological, emphasis emerges, which corresponds to
the *creaturely* Sophia, to the glorification of the creature.
Even more significant are the sophiological symbols
employed to depict divine Sophia in the theology of
color and imagery. Here the most complicated and
involved dogmatic compositions, interpreted only with
difficulty, embody the devout contemplation of the
unknown makers. These icons have been accepted and
authorized by the Church and are preserved to this day.[1]
But these memorials of symbolic sophiology remain
dumb, and though their meaning must have been clear
when they were composed, in our time, which lacks
sophianic inspiration, they often remain enigmatic and
partially incomprehensible relics of a former age. Scholastic theology commonly abandons the whole field of
research into the lofty symbolism of sophianic churches
and icons, together with the appropriate texts of divine

---

1. See the photographs of icons of Sophia in Van der Mensbrugghe,
From Dyad to Triad, London, 1935.

worship, to the realm of archeology, as something essentially antiquated, or else interprets it somewhat unsympathetically as a theological misunderstanding, the result of the unduly elaborate allegorizing of Byzantium or its naive imitation in Russia. This wealth of symbolism has been preserved in the archives of ecclesiastical antiquities, but, covered by the dust of ages, it has been of no use to anyone. The time has come for us to sweep away the dust of ages and to decipher the sacred script, to reinstate the tradition of the Church, in this instance all but broken, as a *living* tradition. It is *holy tradition which lays such tasks upon us.* It is a call neither to superstitious idolatry, nor to rationalistic contempt, but rather to creative understanding and development. Our own particular time with its special revelations and destiny has a peculiar call to this task.

The theme of Sophia never had any place in Western theology, either in the Middle Ages, or at the period of the Reformation, in spite of the intense theological ferment of the time. Though there is no doubt that Western theology constantly hovers on the brink of sophiological problems, the general context of the main problems of the Reformation and the Counter-Reformation, with their exclusive emphasis on questions of personal salvation, of grace and of faith, was on the whole unfavorable to further dogmatic development, and particularly to a consideration of anthropology in its connection with cosmology, which is a special characteristic of sophiology. Protestantism showed itself particularly barren in this sphere, for it narrowed tremendously the whole range of theological problems. This is particularly true of modern Protestantism, both of the "liberal" variety with its rationalistic adogmatism and historicism—*Leben-Jesu-Fors-chung*—and of the "orthodox" variety which reintroduces with new vigor all the limitations of its original world outlook. Unfortunately the sophiological barrenness of Western theology influenced Eastern theology also in a negative direction, for, generally speaking, Eastern theology was subject to influence from this quarter. This resulted in a certain divergence between the true wisdom of the Church on the one hand and the rationalistic forms of theology on the other. Today we are compelled to reestablish the connection.

Quite unexpectedly and apart altogether from any link with the Eastern tradition of the veneration of Sophia, we observe the beginning of teaching on the *Jungfrau Sophia* in the West in the seventeenth century, in the doctrine of Jacob Boehme, the mysterious cobbler of Görlitz. Boehme is perhaps the greatest genius among German thinkers. Together with Eckhart, he represents the secret dynamic of the philosophy of Hegel and Schelling, of F. Baader and the romanticists. He had a tremendous influence on his contemporaries as well as on succeeding generations both in Germany and beyond, for example in England. In particular this applies to his peculiar doctrine of Sophia, which is closely linked with his trinitarian theology. We may here add that an English mystic of the eighteenth century, Dr. Pordage, who wrote a series of remarkable treatises on Sophia, was thus influenced by Boehme's sophiology. This Western sophiology is primarily distinguished by the fact that already at this stage it came to realize the vital nature of the problems involved, and gave rise to a whole range of valuable and penetrating ideas on this subject. Nevertheless it cannot altogether be accepted by modern Orthodox sophiology, though this latter must give it its due. The works of Boehme, Pordage, and others were diligently studied by Russian Freemasons at the end of the eighteenth and the beginning of the nineteenth centuries. The translations of these works, in spite of the prohibition of the censor, were published and read in Russia and undoubtedly had a lasting influence on Russian thought. However, modern Russian teaching on Sophia does not derive from these sources, but from holy tradition, which silently pervades the whole history of the Eastern Church.

We should remember that in the history of Russian religious thought the nineteenth century is characterized by its exceptional sensitiveness to such problems as the religious meaning of history, of creativity, of culture. This theme finds expression in the wording of the title of a work published by one of the earliest representatives of this line of thought, A. M. Bukharev (the Archimandrite Theodore): *Orthodoxy in Its Relation to Our Time*. The questions relating to the religious justification of culture and of creativity which were raised by the Reformation and by humanism and could only find a solution there in secularization, were in turn experienced, and in a far more painful way, by Russian thought. This process occurred, however, not so much within the sphere of official theology, which was insufficiently developed for such a task and was, in addition, fettered by official scholastic orthodoxy, as among the representatives of literature and art. Artistic creativity was deeply conscious of its religious sources. Gogol was literally consumed by his search, and by his attempt to make of the whole of his creative work a true sacrifice offered to God. The life of the Archimandrite Theodore was destined to become a continual tragedy as a result of his prophetic seeking for new ways of life and creativity. This ascetic monk, one of the greatest men of prayer, found himself in spiritual conflict with the ecclesiastical environment in which he lived. He returned to the status of a layman because he found that only by this immense sacrifice could he procure the right to follow freely his own particular way of service.

The problems raised in the works of Gogol and Bukharev are further illumined in a new way in Dostoievsky, with his constant search for the way to that Kingdom of God in the world, which he foresaw as the future destiny of Orthodoxy. Besides this we observe in Dostoievsky a profound feeling for "mother earth," for the cosmic aspect of the Church, together with the anthropological revelation found in the Church, and a vivid apocalyptic interpretation of history. We should also mention in this respect several of our greatest poets who were gifted with special insight into the mysticism of the natural world: especially Tiutchev, the poet of cosmic chaos; Fiet, who was very much akin to him; Baratinsky and others. At a time when the majority of the Russian intelligentsia was carried away by a superficial positivism or, at best, by Tolstoy's limited moralism, a real spiritual renaissance was taking place in Russian Orthodox thought in this small exclusive circle. Yet another such solitary thinker was Fedorov, who bore real marks of greatness in spite of certain paradoxical and enigmatical elements in his makeup; he interpreted Christianity as the "common cause" of the resurrection of the ancestors by their descendants, in the power of Christ, and in the

name of the Holy Trinity. Although in a certain sense isolated, spiritually (and even historically) he undoubtedly
belongs to the general trend of thought.

Toward the end of the nineteenth century this quest at
last begins to find expression in a theology the basic characteristic of which lies in its teaching on Sophia, or sophiology. Vladimir Solovyov (1853-1900), is the first representative of this theology, the first Russian sophiologist. In
his treatise *Lectures on Divine-humanity* [or *"God-manhood"*]
(1877–1881), which was printed in one of the leading
Church journals, he gives a philosophical and theological
formulation of the doctrine of the Wisdom of God. He
expounds his doctrine in numerous articles and books, in
particular in *La Russie et l'église universelle*, 1885. Nevertheless it should be pointed out here that Solovyov's doctrine
of Sophia is undoubtedly syncretistic: side by side with
ancient Orthodox tradition we can detect elements
derived from the ancient gnostic systems, together with
the obvious influence of Western sophiology in the writings of Boehme and others. All this is further complicated by his own poetic mysticism. In his poetry Solovyov
is indeed very far from the Orthodox conception of
Sophia. This aspect of his world outlook had a profound
(and far from valuable) influence on the subsequent generation of poets such as the gifted Blok, Biely, and certain
others, who expound in their poetry themes for the most
part of an erotic-gnostic character concerning the feminine principle. It is also obvious that Vladimir Solovyov
had a tremendous influence on Dostoievsky; this is particularly noticeable in the latter's prophetic utterances concerning "mother earth" and the "free theocracy" of the
future. Solovyov's religious outlook had an inescapable

influence on the thought of subsequent generations, whether those who submitted to it did so consciously or not. Personally, though I do not share his gnostic tendencies, I regard Solovyov as having been my philosophical "guide to Christ" at the time of a change in my own world outlook, when I was moving "From Marxism to Idealism"[2] and, indeed, even further, to the Church.

It is very important to emphasize this general link between Solovyov and all the preceding currents of Russian thought, for his Christian philosophy in a certain sense embraces them all.[3] There is a direct line which leads to Solovyov starting from the Slavophile theology of Khomiakov and continuing through the other thinkers I have mentioned. All the living Russian religious thinkers of our time have been influenced directly or indirectly, positively or negatively, by sophiology, S. N. and E. N. Trubetskoy, Berdyaev, Zenkovsky, Karsavin, Florensky and others. Fr. Paul Florensky, formerly a professor of the Moscow Theological Academy, puts the problem of sophiology in an absolutely Orthodox setting. In his well-known work *The Pillar and Ground of the Truth* (The Church) he gives in the chapter on Sophia an interesting theological interpretation of the facts of iconography and liturgy referred to above, and further illuminates it by his own ecclesiology. This book

---

2. Under this title a symposium of my articles was published in 1895-1903. One of the most prominent places in it is occupied by an article on Solovyov.

3. There is only one peculiarity in Solovyov's outlook which separates him from this tradition, namely, his "Romanizing" recognition of the primacy of the Pope, in which recognition he saw the ancient tradition of the Church.

produced a profound impression in Russian theological thought and led to much discussion. Its sophiological ideas became an inseparable part at any rate of the problems raised by Russian religious thought. I myself have developed my own position in a series of books, at first mainly philosophical, such as *The Philosophy of Economics*, 1912; *The Unfading Light*, 1917; *The Tragedy of Philosophy [Die Tragaedie der Philosophie]*, 1927; and later in a series of theological works published abroad.

Russian religious thought finds itself in an unfortunate position in the Christian world; it is still an undiscovered continent for Christendom as a whole, which remains in a state of blissful ignorance of our "barbarous" tongue (the tongue, however, of some of the greatest writers and of world-famous poets). It is only by chance that certain things from the treasury of Russian thought (by no means the most valuable and authentic) rise to the surface of the spiritual vortex of European life. These strike Europeans as peculiar, so that they go on to ascribe the general spiritual atmosphere which the works share to the individual or the work in question. In the same way the Bolsheviks, when confronted with an ignorant "Intourist," are apt to credit themselves for such things as the Russian winter, the Russian Volga, Russian art, and so forth. From our standpoint, we Russian Europeans, when watching the manifestations of European thought, are often struck by the fact that trends of thought which appear to us elementary, of small importance, and, to be frank, entirely devoid of originality, acquire the significance of historical events and lead to the formation of "schools," producing in time a whole literature. (This, of course, does not apply to purely scientific research, where the predominance of the West is obvious.) But this attitude is particularly irritating to us at the present time in a period of otherwise developing inter-confessional intercourse.

A Russian proverb says, "One cannot love to order"; nevertheless it is at least the duty of Western Christians to *know* us as we are, if only for the reason that so far no other Church has had to experience the fiery trials through which we have passed, together with the spiritual revelations which they conceal. And if the general attitude of the West in relation to Russian thought may still be expressed by the rule *graeca sunt, non leguntur* (they are Greeks, not chosen), we on our part are called to form a sort of "novitiate," endeavoring to render at least the main currents of our thought accessible to the West in some concise form. The present outline of sophiology pursues this course. It has been specially compiled for Western readers with the secret hope of arousing their interest and urging them to become acquainted with the main works bearing on the subject.

The main purport of this essay is to expound the doctrine of Sophia, the Wisdom of God. This doctrine is at the present time responsible for a sort of ideological ferment even in our own Orthodox *milieux*. It has already evoked a hurried condemnation on the part of some of the hierarchy, in spite of the fact that the whole problem is only on the threshold of dogmatic consideration. As a result of the atmosphere of sensation or scandal thus created around the doctrine of the Wisdom of God, Western readers have already become acquainted with such words as "Sophia" and "sophiology." For them, of course, these words are tinged with the peculiar exotic Oriental flavor of "gnosis," and, indeed, smack of every sort of rubbish and superstition. No one seems to suspect that in this controversy the underlying problem is one which has a profound bearing on the very "essence of Christianity," that it is a problem which is even now being discussed by the whole of Western Christendom. The real point at issue is that of the Christian vocation as it is related to the very nature of Christianity; it is the problem of a dogmatic *metanoia*, nothing less than a change and a renewal of human hearts. The doctrine of divine Sophia has nothing to do with putting forward any new dogma, and certainly cannot be described as a new heresy within Christianity, although such is the attitude adopted by certain "guardians" of the faith, who see in complete stagnation the only guarantee of a true faith and dread all new ideas accordingly.

Sophiology represents a theological or, if you prefer, a dogmatic, interpretation of the world (*Weltanschauung*) within Christianity. It is characteristic only of one trend of thought within Christianity, and that one which is by no means dominant in the Orthodox Church, just as, for instance, Thomism or "Modernism" exists within Catholicism, or liberal "Jesuanism" or Barthianism within Protestantism. The sophiological point of view brings a special interpretation to bear upon *all* Christian teaching and dogma, beginning with the doctrine of the Holy Trinity and the Incarnation and ending with questions of practical everyday Christianity in our own time. It is untrue to affirm that the development of the doctrine of the Wisdom of God leads to the denial or undermining of any part of Christian dogma. Exactly the reverse is true. Sophiology accepts all the dogmas acknowledged as genuine by the Orthodox Church (though not those teachings which have been accepted through scholastic misunderstanding, and, frequently, forced on the Church from outside). Wherein, then, does this sophiological point of view consist, and in what way can it be applied to the fundamental teaching of Christianity? This essay is an attempt to give a short answer to this question. The introduction can only indicate quite briefly the general lay of the land.

The central point from which sophiology proceeds is that of the relation between *God* and *the world*, or, what is practically the same thing, between *God* and *humanity*. In other words we are faced with the question of the meaning and significance of Divine-humanity[4]—not only insofar as it concerns the God-human, the incarnate Logos, but precisely insofar as it applies to the theandric union between God and the whole of the creaturely world, through humanity and in humanity. Within Christianity itself there is a neverending struggle between the two extreme positions of dualism and monism, in a constant search for truth, which can only be found in the synthesis of Divine-humanity.

There are two opposite poles in the Christian attitude to life, which are both equally untrue in their one-sidedness. These are, firstly, world-denying Manicheism, which separates God from the world by an impassable gulf and thus makes the existence of Divine-humanity out of the question; and, secondly, an acceptance of the world as it

---

4. This is the title which Vladimir Solovyov gave to his articles on sophiology—*Lectures on Divine humanity [God-manhood]*. I have called my principal theological work in the same way *On Divine-humanity[God-manhood]*: Part I, *The Lamb of God*; Part II, *The Comforter*; Part III, *On Things to Come* (Ecclesiology and eschatology).

is, combined with submission to its values, which is termed "secularization." We notice the former attitude in various, at times very unexpected, combinations, mostly in cases where a profound and serious religious attitude, a sense of the reality of God, confronts humans with an "either, or"—*either* God, *or* the world. Thus in choosing God, humans are constrained to turn away from the world, to despise its works and values, and to leave the world to itself and to its own creativity in a state of alienation from God. We come across such a-cosmism or even anti-cosmism on the one hand in a trend of thought which has historically prevailed in Orthodoxy, in the "pseudo-monastic" outlook on the world, and on the other hand in orthodox Protestantism, which likewise so insists on God's transcendence to the world that the world is in effect deprived of God.

The second attitude or tendency—the secularization of life—only indicates the general spiritual paralysis of modern Christianity, which is, in practice, powerless to direct or to control life. Instead it submits to the existing order of things. Such worship of the status quo shows that it has no answer to the problems of life. Moreover, if "salvation" is interpreted as a flight from the world, and is at the same time associated with a servile attitude toward it, we cannot be surprised that the world turns away more and more from such Christianity, and comes to regard itself and its own life as constituting its own standard of values. Such is modern atheism, which really represents a deification of the world and of human beings, and which is a special form of paganism. It is not, as it frequently claims to be, the *zero* of religion, but a *minus* of Christianity.

Christianity is at present powerless to overcome this cleavage, this gulf between religion and the world which is apparent in modern life, for the gulf exists not only outside, but within Christianity itself. Attempts to coordinate Christianity with life (insofar as, in Roman Catholicism, this is accomplished on the basis of subjecting the world to a powerful organization of the Church) are really nothing more than attempts to amalgamate two incongruous bodies which cannot in fact be united, since each insists on its own exclusiveness or totalitarianism. "Social" Christianity finds itself in the same tragic predicament insofar as it also represents a sort of adaptation, a peculiar form of opportunism, without a *dogma* of its own. It strives to become a sort of "applied" Christianity, a "Nicaea of ethics," to use the phrase of Archbishop Söberblom. But the very conception of "applying" Christianity only confirms the absence of a genuine *dogmatic* Nicaea together with a certain readiness to compromise with life, a retreat from it or coming to terms with it, which is in no sense a creative leadership and inspiration of life. So far Christianity has followed in the train of life, lagging behind, without assuming any leadership. Furthermore, how can one lead in regard to something which one does not accept, in which one does not believe, toward which one's attitude is merely that of missionary adaptation, of philanthropy, or of moralism?

Social Christianity, engrossed with its practical aims, has not yet faced its dogmatic problem, namely, that of justifying the world in God, in contrast to excommunicating it from God, which is what is preached and confessed in practice at the two opposite poles of Christianity, both in the Orthodox Church and in Protestantism. Is there a ladder between heaven and earth and do the angels of God ascend and descend upon it? Or is this ladder only a convenient emergency exit for those who wish to be "saved" by forsaking the world? Is our Lord's Ascension into heaven the very last, and, so to speak, culminating act of our salvation? Or is there something else that follows it, something new, in the second coming of Christ into the world, the Parousia, which is not only judgment but at the same time the beginning of a new, eternal abiding of our Lord on earth?

The answer to these questions has been given long ago in the Christian faith, but it has remained a dead letter; it has not, so to speak, become a living reality. This answer is contained in the fundamental dogma of Christianity concerning Divine-humanity. The creaturely world is united with the divine world in divine Sophia. Heaven stoops toward earth; the world is not only a world in itself, it is also the world in God, and God abides not only in heaven but also on earth with human beings. Our Lord says of himself: "All power is given unto me in heaven and in earth" (Matt. 28.18). Divine-humanity represents a dogmatic call both to spiritual ascesis and to creativity, to salvation from the world and to a salvation of the world. This is the dogmatic banner which should be henceforth unfurled with all power and glory in the Church of Christ.

The dogma of Divine-humanity is precisely the main theme of sophiology, which in fact represents nothing but its full dogmatic elucidation. Why exactly this is associated with the doctrine concerning the Wisdom of God and how this connection applies will become evident to the reader in the course of the present work, which gives a short summary of the doctrine of sophiology as it is developed by the author, and will act as a guide to his larger works.

Our modern age stands in need of a new apprehension of the dogmatic formulae preserved by the Church in its living tradition. Moreover it cannot be overemphasized that there is no single dogmatic problem that does not at present need such reinterpretation. And at the very heart of things stands, as of old, the basic Christian dogma of the Incarnation, of the Word made flesh, in the dogmatic setting bequeathed to us by Chalcedon. The roots of this dogma penetrate to the very heart of heaven and earth, into the inmost depths of the Holy Trinity and into the creaturely nature of human beings. "Incarnationism" even now stands as the main fact of dogmatic self-determination in Anglicanism, and in Protestantism also—let alone in the most ancient Churches such as the Orthodox and the Roman Catholic. Do people, however, sufficiently realize that this dogma in itself is not primary, but derived? In itself it presupposes the existence of absolutely necessary dogmatic assumptions in the doctrine of God and humanity, of the primordial Divine-humanity. These presuppositions are in fact unfolded in sophiology. The same applies to an even greater extent to another dogma of Divine-humanity, namely, that of Pentecost. This dogma, though accepted, remains comparatively speaking but feebly elucidated in dogmatic thought. It involves the descent and the abiding of the Holy Spirit in the world in connection with the Incarnation. This connection as well as the power of Pentecost in the one Divine-humanity is also disclosed by sophiology.

To go even further, the fundamental and still insurmountable difficulty so far in our age in the striving of the churches toward unity is the lack of dogma concerning the essence of the Church as such. We are not concerned for the moment with the external attributes of the Church, its canonical or liturgical aspects, but with what the Church *is* in itself. What do we mean by the reunion of the churches in one Church? Is this a "pact" or an act that is a manifestation of the one Church as a revelation of Divine-humanity, as Sophia the Wisdom of God? Until the consciousness of the Church can reach this depth of self-determination, all ecumenical "pacts" will be in vain. Again and again will the separated churches dash in vain against the walls which divide them, in a tragic realization of their helplessness, in face of the objective impossibility of genuine reunion. There is, nevertheless, one true way, which is that of learning to know and understand the Church as revealed Divine-humanity, Sophia the Wisdom of God.

We will not refer here to the numerous theological questions of a more special nature, which acquire a new light in the doctrine of the Wisdom of God. We will confine ourselves to mentioning one more. Never before has the Christian conscience been so pressingly confronted with questions concerning humanity's destiny in history and beyond its limits, humanity's creativity and its responsibility to its own Divine-humanity. History unfolds itself before us as an apocalypse; the apocalypse as eschatology; the "end" as fulfillment; our Lord's second coming in the Parousia as his meeting with the Church: "And the spirit and the bride say, Come! Even so, come Lord Jesus!" (Rev. 22.17, 20).

Are the curses of secularization and the anemic Manichean denial of the world symptoms of weakness, of the
"failure" of historical Christianity, or are they but the
darkness before the dawn, which awaits the rising sun of
the coming day? Is world Divine-humanity in process of
accomplishment, the Wisdom of God becoming manifest, the "woman clothed with the sun" (Rev. 12.1) even
though still driven by the dragon into the wilderness, or
is the world itself only a wilderness, "the empty house,"
forsaken by the Lord?

Two forces struggle in the world in the guise of two
basic tendencies, that of cosmism and that of anti-
cosmism, the two disintegrated aspects of the one divine-
human theocosmism. Historically, secularization was
introduced into the world by the Reformation and the
Renaissance, which represent two parallel turbulent
streams of the same main current—of what we may call,
however contradictory such a definition may sound, anti-
cosmic cosmism. The acceptance of the world by humanism was a reaction against its nonacceptance, which only
left it a right to natural existence. We are confronted in
this process by a bad "dialectic" of unresolved contradic-
tions, which burdens and exhausts our time.

But such a "dialectic" in no sense represents the last
word of wisdom. We need a true Christian ascesis in relation to the world, which consists in a struggle with the
world out of love for the world. We must discover how we
can overcome the secularizing forces of the Reformation
and the Renaissance, not in a negative way or "dialectically," which is in any case merely theoretical and powerless, but in a positive way—through love for the world.
But again we repeat that this can be accomplished only

through a change in our conception of the world, and through a sophianic perception of the world in the Wisdom of God. This alone can give us strength for new inspiration, for new creativity, for the overcoming of the mechanization of life and of human beings. The future of living Christianity rests with the sophianic interpretation of the world and of its destiny. All the dogmatic and practical problems of modern Christian dogmatics and ascetics seem to form a kind of knot, the unraveling of which inevitably leads to sophiology. For this reason, in the true sense of the word, sophiology is a theology of *crisis*, not of disintegration, but of salvation.

And finally, in contemplating culture which has succumbed to secularization and paganism, which has lost its inspiration and has no answer to give to the tragedy of history, which seems in fact to have lost all meaning—we realize that we can find a spring of living water only by a renewal of our faith in the sophianic, or theandric, meaning of the historical process. As the dome of St. Sophia in Constantinople with prophetic symbolism portrays heaven bending to earth, so the Wisdom of God itself is spread like a canopy over our sinful though still hallowed world.

◆

1

The Divine Sophia
in the Holy Trinity[1]

The dogma of the Holy Trinity consists in two basic postulates. The first affirms the triune character of the Deity,
"trinity in unity" and "unity in trinity." The Father, the
Son, and the Holy Spirit, who are three distinct divine
persons, together constitute one God. The second postulate is concerned with the consubstantiality of the Holy
Trinity, which has but one substance or nature *(ousia* or
physis, substantia or *natura.)* This dogma is most clearly
expressed in a Latin Creed of the fifth century, the *Quin-
cunque Vult,* the so-called Athanasian Creed, whose authority is recognized by the Eastern as well as by the Western Church.[2]

---

1. See my previous studies on this subject *The Unfading Light, Chapters on
the Trinity; Hypostasis and Hypostatic Nature* (from the Symposium in honor
of P. B. Struve); *On Divine-humanity [God-manhood]*: Part I, *The Lamb of
God,* Ch. I, para. 2-3, pp. 117-130; Part II, *The Comforter,* para. 1-6, p. 6-63.

2. ... *let us worship one God in a trinity, and the trinity in (a) unity, neither
confusing the persons nor separating (their) substance. For the person of the Father
is one, that of the Son another, that of the Holy Spirit another; but the divinity of the
Father, the Son, and the Holy Spirit is one, the(ir) glory is equal the(ir) majesty is
coeternal.*

The first part of the dogma, that is, the doctrine of the relationship between the three hypostases with their hypostatic qualities and distinctive features, has been to a certain extent elucidated in the process of the Church's dogmatic creativity. But the other side, the doctrine of the consubstantiality of the Holy Trinity, as well as the actual conception of substance or nature, has been far less developed and, apparently, almost overlooked.

Moreover, we should note here that whereas we find the names of the three persons of the Holy Trinity in the Bible, the actual expressions "substance" or "consubstantiality" are not biblical. The term was brought forward and used at the Council of Nicaea as the result of great dogmatic activity, in the endeavor to find in his consubstantiality (homoöusios) with the Father a suitable expression for the idea of the divinity of the Logos. Later this term was extended to the whole Trinity, and the usage became well established in the theology of the Cappadocian fathers, particularly of St. Basil the Great. Still later its use became general in the Eastern Church, and it was largely employed by St. John of Damascus.

The term itself is adapted from the philosophy of Aristotle, who distinguishes between the "first" and the "second" substance in things: between the *concrete* being, in

---

2. *(continued)* The dogma of the consubstantiality of the Holy Trinity is expressed in different ways in the Orthodox liturgy. As an illustration we may notice the two following "ejaculations" of the priest:

1. "Glory be to the Holy, Consubstantial, Life-giving, and Undivided Trinity now and for ever. . . ."

2. "For Thine is the Kingdom, the power and the glory, of the Father, and of the Son, and of the Holy Spirit. . . ."

which the essence, comprising certain "universals," becomes specifically individuated, and the *abstract* concept of essence, devoid of such specific character, and therefore lacking such real being of its own. Aristotle applies this scheme to all individual being, whether it be a stone or an angel, a thing or a human being. The same method is applied by St. Basil the Great and St. John of Damascus to the elucidation of the doctrine of the Holy Trinity, the one divine essence being here individuated in three hypostatic relations, fatherhood, generation and procession. Meanwhile in Western theology (with Augustinianism) the substance or essence in itself, yields precedence to the three hypostases, these being determined in their being through an interrelationship of origin (as opposed one to another).

We thus see that substance both in the East and in the West is interpreted purely as a philosophical abstraction, and utilized to achieve a logical solution of the trinitarian dogma. "Substance" provides doctrinal construction with a kind of ideological starting point. Such a conception cannot embrace the divine revelation with regard to the one common life of the Holy Trinity, of God in three persons. The dogma of consubstantiality, which safeguards the unity of the Holy Trinity, thus remains a sealed book so far as we are concerned—for in a religious sense it has been neither assimilated nor unfolded.

The Bible, however, though it never alludes to the abstract conception of substance, does give us revealed teaching on the life of the triune God. In point of fact this teaching seems to have been little noticed and most certainly has not been utilized in trinitarian theology, in particular as regards the application to the doctrine of the substance of God of the biblical revelation of Wisdom or Sophia, and of the Glory of God. In this particular respect the liturgical consciousness of the Church is superior to the dogmatic, for the earliest liturgical texts have included such revelation in the text of hymns, lessons, and doxologies.[3] The *lex orandi* (law of praying, prayer) bore witness in itself to the *lex credendi* (law of belief, believing). This witness, however, was disregarded by theology until the middle of the nineteenth century in Russia, when there were fresh stirrings of sophiological though.

We find teaching about the Wisdom of God (*he Sophia tou Theou*), or Hochmah (Hebrew), in the first instance in Proverbs. Chapters 1–10 obviously make use of this term to express wisdom as a quality—1.7; 2.6, 10; 3.13, 14-18; 4.5; 7.4; 9.10. There is a double meaning in 1.22-23 and 3.19-20. But there is no longer any doubt that 8.22-31 contains an interpretation of wisdom as somehow divine and quasi-hypostatic, though not a person.[4] There are no adequate reasons for equating this principle with the Logos, the second Hypostasis, as was done in Arian and anti-Arian patristic exegesis. Nevertheless, this principle is *with* God and is prior to the world. "The Lord possessed me in the beginning of his way, before his

---

3. Even the Athanasian Creed, as we have already seen, speaks of *una divinitas, aequalis gloria, coaeterna maiestas* (one divinity, equal glory, coeternal majesty). These expressions, however, have something of a rhetorical air, and are not usually interpreted as authoritative dogmatic formulae.

4. "Wisdom is personal, but not a person." (Drummond: *A New Commentary on Holy Scripture*, II, 70).

works of old," 8.22, it is therefore coeternal with God ("I was set up from everlasting, from the beginning, or ever the earth was" 8.23, *et seq.*). Wisdom belongs to God "in the beginning of his way," as "a wise master-workman," and is his joy; its delights are to be with the sons of men (30-31). We see a similar conception of the Wisdom of God in Job 28.20-27. Prov. 9.I-4, also speaks of Wisdom in this personified way, though this text seems to have a double meaning.

We find an ontological interpretation of Wisdom in the two pseudepigrapha, the Wisdom of Solomon and the Wisdom of Jesus Ben-Sirach (Ecclesiastes). These together form a sort of metaphysical commentary on Proverbs. In the wisdom of Solomon, in addition to 1:5, 8, chapter 7 is of fundamental significance. It treats of Wisdom, the master-workman of all, (*he ton panton tech-netes*), as also of the "spirit of Wisdom." She is the "breath of the power of God, a pure influence flowing from the glory of the Almighty," (*tas ton pantokratoros doxes*). She is the "brightness of the everlasting light, the unspotted mirror of the power of God (*tou theou energe-ias*) and the image of his goodness." "She is conversant with God," and is "privy to the mysteries of the knowledge of God." By Wisdom the Lord has made human beings (*kataskenasas anthropon*). Wisdom "knows thy works for it was present with thee, when thou didst create the world." Chapters 10–12 represent Wisdom not only as the power which was present before the world came into being, but as a power which continually protects and preserves it.

Wisdom is portrayed in the same way in Ecclesiasticus. Chapters 1 and 24 sing the praises of Sophia: (*ainesis*

Sophias)—"All wisdom cometh from the Lord, and is with him for ever" (1-1); "I came out of the mouth of the most high, and covered the earth as a cloud" (243). Without going into detail we may say that the striking figure which conveys this teaching on wisdom obviously does not admit of being interpreted in the sense of quality or attribute, for this would destroy the figure itself. But here we should notice yet another point. Though we must disregard the obviously inadmissible interpretation of Wisdom as the Second Hypostasis, or the Logos,[5] yet we must at the same time recognize that the principle of Wisdom has never received satisfactory theological interpretation or application, so that even today it is overlooked by theology and only succeeds in creating misunderstanding. It is impossible, however, that this should always remain the case.

A few words now on the manner in which the conception of Wisdom is applied in the New Testament. We will not consider here the comparatively numerous texts in which wisdom is definitely to be understood as a property (2 Pet. 3.15; Rom. 11.33; 1 Cor. 1.17, 20-30; Eph. 1.8, 17; 3.10; Col. 1.9, 28; 2.3; 3.16; Rev. 5.12; 7.12). We have a passage (1 Cor. 1.24), where this principle is applied christologically (cp. Luke 11.49), but we also observe that it is used without any relation to Christology in Matt. 11.19 and Luke 7.35. But even this christological adaptation

---

5. The Arian interpretation was based upon the phrase "God created *ektisa*, wisdom." This is, however, more accurately rendered now as *ektesato* "had," "possessed," "formed me" (22). It is true that verse 24 reads "gives birth to me," *genna me* ("I was brought forth" or "I was fashioned"). But if we compare this expression with v. 22 we shall see that it cannot be regarded as having a dogmatic reference to the Son.

should be understood in the light of, and in connection with, Old Testament sophiology (see below).

We thus observe in biblical theology side by side with a revelation of the personal being of God, a doctrine of divine Wisdom either in God or with God. But alongside the idea of Wisdom we see in the Old Testament also yet another striking figure, namely, that of the Shekinah, the Glory of God, in the midst of which God manifests himself. We meet this for the first time in Exod. 16.7-10: "Ye shall see the Glory of the Lord . . . and, behold, the Glory of the Lord appeared in the cloud." (5 Lev. 9.16, 23; Numb. 14.10; 16.19, 42; 22.6.) The Glory of the Lord fills the tabernacle like a cloud (Exodus 40.34-35, cp. Numb. 9.15-23); similarly Solomon's Temple (1 Kings 8.10-11; 2 Chron. 5.13-14). God's appearance to Moses on Mount Sinai has, of course, a very special significance. This also took place in a cloud of Glory. Exod. 24.16-18, and especially 33.18-23, describe how Moses, in fulfillment of his desire, was allowed to behold the Glory of God, and in this instance a vision of the Glory of God is contrasted with a vision of the "Face" of the Lord. The vision of Glory itself is described as: "And the Lord descended in the cloud, and stood with him there, and proclaimed the name of the Lord. And the Lord passed by before him, and proclaimed, 'The Lord, the Lord, a God full of compassion and gracious, slow to anger, and plenteous in mercy and truth'" (34.5-6). In this passage (33.22-23) two comparisons are drawn simultaneously. On the one hand the Glory is contrasted with the Face of God, to wit, his hypostatic revelation; on the other hand, the manifestation of Glory is identified with the manifestation of God himself, shown by the proclamation of God's name.

God's manifestation of himself to Moses may be compared with his manifestation to another great prophet, Elijah, who subsequently, together with Moses, was a witness of Christ's Glory on the Mount of Transfiguration. God manifests himself to Elijah on Mount Horeb, no longer in a cloud, but in a "still small voice" (1 Kings 19.12). Then follows the great prophet Isaiah, who sees a vision of the Lord on his throne: "and his train filled the temple" (Isa.6.1). . . *tes doxes.* Finally we get the most monumental figure of God's Glory in the vision of Ezekiel (1–2), who speaks of his vision of Glory as something sensibly perceptible taking place in a definite place and at a definite time, as something which moves, comes nearer or withdraws: 3.12–13; 8.4; 9.3; 11.22–23; 40.2–5. At present there is no need for us to analyze the particular details of the appearance of Ezekiel's chariot in all its complexity. It is an "image of the Glory of God."

If we compare all these visible manifestations of the Glory of God, we are inevitably led to ask, what does it mean in its relation to God? In this case, indeed, we are not faced with the temptation—which, as a matter of history, has been felt in relation to wisdom—to interpret this Glory as either a created principle or a "property" of God. The Glory of God in these instances is obviously intended to represent a divine principle. Though it differs from God's *personal* being, yet it is inseparably bound up with it: it is not God, but divinity.

The same thing could be said about Glory that has already been said about Wisdom, which is that this conception has not only failed to receive any theological interpretation, but seems to have been completely passed over in dogmatics. The following tentative conclusion can be drawn on the basis of the comparisons made above. God has, or possesses, or is characterized by, Glory and Wisdom, which cannot be separated from him since they represent his dynamic self-revelation in creative action, and also in his own life. Moreover, it should be added that the Face of God, which remains hidden in the Old Testament, is in the New Testament unveiled in its tri-personal nature. Hence we must conclude that the divine "substances" in question also belong to the Holy Trinity, for the sacred text gives us no grounds for limiting them to any one particular person of the Holy Trinity—for example, to the Father or to the Son.[6]

What then is the relation between the dogmatic conception of divine substance or nature (*ousia* or *physis*) and the figurative revelations of the Bible bearing on the one hand on Wisdom (*Sophia*) and on the other on Glory? Is there any ground for distinguishing and contrasting them? In the first place, is there any reason for differentiating between Wisdom and Glory, as two distinct principles within the Godhead in its self-revelation, or its revelation to creation respectively? There is no doubt whatever that they do differ from each other as two distinct aspects of the Godhead in its revelation: Wisdom, the first, concerns its content; Glory, the second, its manifestation. Nevertheless, these two distinct aspects can in no way be separated from each other or

---

6. The Arians and the anti-Arians who attempted to equate wisdom with the Son, by their very attempt deny wisdom both to the Father and to the Holy Spirit. The misunderstandings which arise from 1 Cor. 1.24 will be considered later on.

replaced by one another, as two principles within the Godhead. This would contradict the truth of monotheism, for the one personal God possesses but one Godhead, which is expressed at once in Wisdom and Glory. The fact of there being two figures does not make two Godheads, however much these figures may differ from each other. This doubling of the figures is due to their peculiar nature, though this does not in any way minimize the fact that they are identical in substance. The Holy Bible, however, is not concerned with systematic theology. It presents us with its similitudes in the form of theological raw material, so to speak. It is the task of biblical theology to understand and to compare these similitudes.

Let us consider next what sort of relationship can exist between the abstract Aristotelian *ousia* or substance, the principle of consubstantiality within the Holy Trinity (according to the recognized dogmatic definition), and the Wisdom and Glory which we find in the Bible. Perhaps, it may be said, there is no relationship between them (and as a matter of fact, in actual practice, theology has so far tacitly answered the question in precisely this way, for it has failed to observe the existence of any relationship at all). However, to state this question directly is enough to realize how impossible is such a solution. The denial of the existence of any connection between Ousia on the one hand, and Wisdom-Glory on the other, undoubtedly creates a dualism in the Godhead. If Ousia differs radically from the concrete figures which depict the life of the Godhead in Wisdom and Glory, then it becomes an empty, abstract metaphysical schema. Monotheism, therefore, necessarily postulates the identity of the two principles—the dogmatic and the biblical. In a certain sense, which will be shortly defined, ousia stands precisely for Wisdom and Glory, "even his eternal Power and Godhead" (Rom. 1.20).[7]

It is possible, of course, for the sake of simplicity in terminology, to fuse this triad of definitions, Ousia= Sophia=Glory, and express its significance by any one of the three terms at random. But the actual history of dogmatic thought is hostile to such terminological anarchy, for every one of these expressions is associated with a definite shade of meaning. In practice, therefore, we should not restrict the circle of sophiological problems to the single term Ousia. Such a procedure would be useless when we come to consider the place occupied in the history of dogma by this particular dogmatic precision. On the contrary it seems much more natural to link the problems of our own time with the term "Sophia" (further amplified by the term "Glory"). Yet still, using an abridged and simplified terminology, we can say: the divinity in God constitutes the divine Sophia (or glory), while at the same time we assume that it is also the ousia: Ousia=Sophia=Glory.

We are next faced with the question of how to conceive of the Godhead in reference to its hypostatic aspect. The tri-hypostatic God possesses, indeed, but one

---

7. We see an analogy in the history of dogma when the Eastern Church accepted the teaching of St. Gregory of Palamas (fourteenth century) which regards the Godhead as a Divine Ousia possessing energies, *energeiai*. This teaching regards the transcendent Ousia and the multiform energies which serve to reveal it as equivalent, in spite of the differences between them. We have a similar "equivalence in difference" in the case of Ousia, on the one hand, and Wisdom and Glory, on the other.

Godhead, Sophia; possesses it in such a way that at the same time it belongs to each of the persons, in accordance with the properties distinguishing each of these persons (just in the same way as each one possesses the one common Ousia).[8] Ousia-Sophia is distinct from the hypostases, though it cannot exist apart from them and is eternally hypostatized in them. Thus Sophia is distinguished by the capacity of belonging to the hypostasis, of being included, that is, in the hypostatic being, which nevertheless appears to be quite compatible with its own un-hypostatic nature. God is Spirit, and it is an attribute of Spirit to possess a hypostasis which abides in its own nature, or to be the subject of its own nature, which is a unity of predicates, in such a way that their mutual relationship and connection expresses the life of the Spirit. But this very life in itself takes for granted the fact that the nature of spirit is not a thing, but a living principle, even though it is not personal. Ousia-Sophia is the life of a hypostatic spirit, though not itself hypostatic.

But what is it that permeates the life of the Godhead? In other words, what *is* God? God is Love—not love in the sense of a quality or a property peculiar to God, but as the very substance and vigor of his life. The tri-hypostatic union of the Godhead is a mutual love, in which each of the hypostases, by a timeless act of self-giving in love, reveals itself in both the others. However, the divine hypostases alone do not constitute the only personal centers of this love, for Ousia-Sophia likewise belongs to the

---

8. Cf. Augustine, *de Trin.*, I, VII, c. I-III: *Ergo et Pater ipse Sapientia est.... Unde et Pater et Filius simul una Sapientia est, quia una essentia....* (*Therefore the Father too is himself wisdom.... whence both the Father and the Son are at the same time together wisdom, because their essence is one....*)

realm of God's Love. It is loved by the Holy Trinity as life and revelation, in it the triune God loves himself. But its own being in relation to the divine person cannot be defined as no more than the mere fact of being their common possession. On the contrary, it too is love, though love in a special and un-hypostatic embodiment. Love is multiform: the aspects of love in the Trinity vary in each of the persons. But besides that which is personal there can be a love which is not.[9] All life in God, in itself, is love. In this sense we can speak of love in God not only in the mutual relationship of the three hypostases and in the relationship of God to his Godhead, but in like manner in the love of the Godhead for God. Thus if God loves Sophia, Sophia also loves God. Apart from this the tri-hypostatic relation between God and his Ousia is inconceivable.

To sum up, the nature of God (which is in fact Sophia) is a living and, therefore, loving substance, ground, and "principle." But, it might be said, does this not lead to the conception of a "fourth hypostasis"? The reply is "certainly not," for this principle in itself is non-hypostatic, though capable of being hypostatized in a given Hypostasis, and thereby constituting its life. But, it might still be urged, would this not result in "another God," a sort of totally "other" divine principle within God? Again we

---

9. A wide range of texts from the Bible, bearing on the love of nature for its Creator (Ps. 19, 1–5, Ps. 148), the love of the Church for Christ (Eph. 4.11; 5.32; Rev. 21.9; 22.17), and others, and similarly a great number of Orthodox liturgical texts speak of the existence of such an un-hypostatic, passive form of love. Apart from such an interpretation all these expressions lose their whole significance and become rhetorical metaphors. The general meaning of these texts is that nature praises God, that is, loves the Creator with a special non-hypostatic love.

reply, no; for no one has ever attempted to maintain such an idea in connection with the divine Ousia in its relation to the hypostases,[10] while the very conception of Ousia itself is but that of Sophia, less fully developed. The whole strength of the dogma of the Holy Trinity lies in this insistence on the one life and one substance of the divine tri-unity, as well as on their mutual identity: God possesses the Godhead, or he *is* the Godhead, is Ousia, Sophia. This does not imply that the three persons own in common, and separately make use of, a certain common substance—on the basis, so to speak, of collective ownership. This would lead to tritheism, not trinitarianism. The living tri-unity of the Holy Trinity is founded on a single principle of self-revelation with one life in common, though in three distinct persons. The Holy Trinity has one Ousia, not three, or three-thirds of an Ousia divided up between the three persons. It likewise possesses one Wisdom, not three, one Glory, not three. Thus of its own accord falls to the ground the first misconception which arises on the very threshold of sophiology.

10. The teaching of Gilbert de la Porrée, which was condemned by the Council of Rheims in 1147, contained the idea that the nature of the Godhead constitutes a fourth term within the Trinity, which is thus rather *quaternitas*. The Council very justly proclaimed that *Divinitas sit Deus et Deus Divinitas* (*Divinity is God and God is Divinity*). [*See* St. Bernard, *in Cantica, Sermo* LXXX. Tr.]

2

The Divine Sophia and
the Persons of the Holy Trinity

The Holy Trinity is consubstantial and indivisible. The three persons of the Holy Trinity have one life in common, that is, one Ousia, one Sophia. Nevertheless this *unity* of divine life coexists with the fact that the life of each of the hypostases in the divine Ousia-Sophia is determined in accordance with its own personal character, or specific hypostatic features. One and the same Sophia is possessed *in a different way* by the Father, the Son, and the Holy Spirit, and this threefold "otherness" is reflected in our definition of Sophia. We should learn to think of the divine Sophia as at the same time threefold and one. The divine tri-unity is mirrored in her with all its characteristics. There is, however, a difference to be observed in logical emphasis when interpreting on the one hand the *tri*-unity of the *three* hypostases, and on the other the tri-*unity* of the single divine Sophia. In the first case we are contemplating the personal hypostases of the Holy Trinity, which differ from one another—*three* which are one; in the second instance, there is only the one substance, whose being is determined in a threefold manner. The tri-unity of the hypostases is reflected in the threefold modality of the one Ousia-Sophia of the Godhead.

Let us now consider in more detail this threefold character of the divine Sophia. In the process we shall discover that this threefold character, which arises from the fact that the divine Sophia belongs to all three hypostases, is a basic principle. Now there is a curious sort of prejudice in regard to sophiology, to the effect that Sophia can be associated only with one hypostasis, namely, that of the Son, an association which practically amounts to identification. This conclusion is based on an erroneous interpretation of 1 Cor. 1.24 (with which we shall deal later). The acceptance of such an interpretation would necessarily imply (as St. Augustine pointed out), that the Father himself is without wisdom, as also is the Holy Spirit, who is the very "Spirit of Wisdom." This is obviously absurd. The problem has been oversimplified at the cost of being confused. Unitarianism is thus introduced into sophiology, in place of the trinitarian principle. Insofar as Sophia is a counterpart of Ousia, she is akin to the whole of the Holy Trinity and to all its three hypostases, both as separate persons and in their mutual association.

In the first place, Wisdom belongs to the Father, who is the "First Principle," or the hypostasis disclosed in the dyad of the two revealing hypostases, that is, of the Son and of the Holy Spirit. The Father[1] represents the

---

1. See *The Comforter*, the epilogue: "The Father" (p. 406 and following). Compare also *Die Tragaedie der Philosophie*.

transcendental principle within the Holy Trinity, he who does not reveal himself but is revealed insofar as he is immanent in the other hypostases which reveal him. He is, so to speak, the divine subject, the subject which manifests itself in the predicate. He constitutes the divine depth and mystery. He represents, as it were, that speechless silence which is presupposed by the Word. He is intelligence contemplating itself (*noesis tes nueseos*)—even "before" the articulation of its thought. He is the primal will, the principle of all volition, the fullness participated by all being. He comprises the unity of all, and is prior to all distinction. He is the source of beauty, which must exist before beauty can come to be. He is love, although this love is withheld within himself and as yet unmanifested. He is the Father, the source of being and of love, that love which cannot but diffuse itself.

But this principle of transcendence does not exist in the abstract, shut up within itself, as it were, for it is inseparably united with the immanent (in a bond of love). The transcendent constitutes the ground and source of the immanent, and the immanent cannot exist without a *point d'appui* in the transcendent. In the personal life of the Holy Trinity this corresponds to the relationship which exists between the hypostasis who reveals himself and those who reveal him, in their mutual association. The Holy Trinity itself is a relationship of mutual self-revelation (though not of causal "origin" in the sense of emergence, as this is usually interpreted).

The Father begets the Word and abides in him by the Holy Spirit who proceeds from the Father. The Father is thus disclosed in this bi-hypostatic unity, in the dyad of

Son and Holy Spirit. In this process the self-revelation of
the Father is absolutely complete, for the Father represents the transcendent in the hypostases who reveal him
and who correspond to the immanent principle in the
Godhead. Within the Holy Trinity itself there is no room
for any undisclosed mystery: "God is light and in him is
no darkness at all" (1 John 1.5). The Father does not
keep back in himself anything which has not already
been manifested in the Son, and fulfilled in the Holy
Spirit: "As the Father knoweth me, even so know I the
Father" (John 10.15) says the Son of himself. In a similar
way it is said of the Spirit: "For the Spirit searcheth all
things, yea, the deep things of God" (1 Cor. 2.7;10.11).
Therefore the Father is mystery abiding in itself, yet disclosed in the dyad of the Son and Spirit.

The unity of the divine Ousia-Sophia is such that the
Father possesses her first of all in the tri-unity of the
Holy Trinity and therefore in common with the Son and
the Holy Spirit. However, in his personal, hypostatic
being, he possesses her as a *source* of revelation, as the
mystery and depth of his hypostatic being, in a true
sense as his own nature—*natura*—which has still to be
manifest, and is to be disclosed in the hypostases which
reveal him. Insofar as the Father permits the revealing
hypostases to disclose her, the divine Sophia abides in
the Father primarily as Ousia, the undisclosed depth of
his nature. But this primordial divine darkness is identical with that "light which no man can approach unto" (1
Tim. 6.16), wherein God dwells. For "God is light and in
him is no darkness at all" (1 John 1.5). Thus, the
hypostasis of the Father in himself remains undisclosed,
for he is only revealed in the other hypostases by the

power of his self-denying sacrificial love. And in the same way his Ousia abides within him, unrevealed, in the capacity of Sophia. This relationship may be expressed by the following formula: Sophia so far as the hypostasis of the Father is concerned, connotes predominantly Ousia—prior to its own revelation as Sophia.

Now let us turn to the Second Hypostasis, that of the Logos, and his relationship to the Father. In the Logos we have a hypostasis which directly reveals the Father, the hypostatic Word of the Father. The general relationship existing between him who speaks the Word of God and the uttered Word itself has been sufficiently expounded in Holy Scripture and in theology. The Son is the Word of the Father, the image and radiance of his glory, his revelation in the Word. The Logos is the proper hypostasis of the Word in all the plenitude of the *ancient* meaning of that term: namely, the Word-thought, Logos-logic, intelligence contemplating itself, both the thinker and the thought, intelligence hypostatized. Even within the hypostasis of the Word himself we can distinguish between the transcendent and the immanent principles, the subject and the predicate, him who speaks and what is spoken: the hypostatic Word itself which speaks and the Word of words spoken, or the content of the Word. This Word spoken constitutes part of the hypostatic life of the Logos in his Ousia. It is precisely this content of divine thought which is disclosed in the hypostasis of the Word in the form of Sophia, or the divine Wisdom. It is this content in particular which touches and embraces everything: "All things were made by him; and without him was not any thing made that was made" (John 1.3). The universal nature of the Word is here expressed not only positively, but reinforced by the negation. How then can we contemplate this *all* understood as the Word of all words, as the content of divine Wisdom, of Ousia, manifested as Sophia?

In the first place we must eliminate any *abstract* interpretation of the words of the Word. According to such abstract interpretation, words are but powerless, lifeless symbols. They possess no vigor of being, for they are only "abstracted" from some other alogical type of being—from "objects." It is quite obvious, however, that we cannot think of any alogical form of being, or of any being outside logic, which would at the same time be an object for, or stand toward, the Logos himself as something given. The words of the Word in themselves possess reason and life. They are, as it were, certain intelligible essences, which can best be described as, like the Platonic *ideas*, ideal and real at the same time, and endowed with the power of life. *Everything* is included in the world of divine being, considered from the point of view of its divine content. It is in this sense that this all comprises the Truth of being and the being of Truth, of which the Word himself says: "I am the way, the truth, and the life" (John 14.6).

We should now adapt what we have said concerning the hypostatic nature of the Word to the definition of the divine Ousia-Sophia, in the aspect which it acquires in relation to the Second Hypostasis. If the words of the Word about *everything* are not mere impotent abstractions, if they are light and life, *ens realissimum* (the most real being), the divine ideas of all being, then this being is the divine Ousia, but Ousia disclosed and manifested as

Sophia, the Wisdom of the divine world, the ideal ground of each distinct specific being. If the Logos is usually described as the Image of the Father's hypostasis, then Sophia as the Ousia in the Logos represents the image of this Image, its objective self-revelation. She stands for the wisdom and the truth of all that is worthy of participating in divine being, namely, of *everything that exists*, since we cannot conceive of the existence of any source of being other than or opposed to the divine. All the manifold forms of being, as many as, having their own specific character, possess a word or an idea, are thereby included in the content of the divine Sophia. This content includes everything, and nothing is excluded from it. It embraces within itself all and everything, all the full-ness—the manifold Wisdom of God—*polypoikilos [wisdom of many colors] Sophia tou Theou* (Eph. 3.10).

It is equally important for us both to identify the Logos in his hypostatic being with this Wisdom, and to distinguish them from each other. Sophia does not exist apart from her connection with the hypostasis of the Logos, without being hypostatized in him: equally the hypostasis of the Logos does not exist apart from his connection with Sophia. Nevertheless, in spite of the indissolubility of their connection we must never lose sight of the distinc-tion between the two. [2] The divine Wisdom consists not only of the Word which proceeds from the "lips of God,"

---

2. For this reason the widespread opinion, based on an insufficient un-derstanding of 1 Cor. 1.24, which simply identifies the hypostatic Logos with Sophia, conflicts radically with the main dogma of the Trinity, which *distinguishes* between Hypostasis and Ousia in God, and conse-quently also in the Logos, between the "uttered" Word, or the hypostatic Word, and his content.

and from "the lips" of the Logos, but also of the Word itself, the content possessing a life of its own. Within the divine Word, the Word and its being cannot be separated or contrasted, for the Word contains words about that which exists, the one Word which embraces all, which is in all and concerns all—"For of him and through him, and to him are all things" (Rom. 11.36). This refers not only to their creation, but also to their eternal preexistence in the divine Sophia.

But if this is the case, if Sophia represents the objective principle which is mutually related to the hypostatic Logos, and is hypostatized in him, then we must establish in this particular case a mutual interrelationship of *love*. This will be the love of the hypostatic Word for his Word of words—for Sophia. It is the love of the divine hypostasis of the Logos for his own self-revelation, for his own divinity. At the same time, this self-revelation constitutes the revelation of the Father in the Son.

The inner connection between the words of *the all* is also the inspiration of love, and not only "logical" association. Different aspects of love—both hypostatic and non-hypostatic—diffuse their radiance here. "Logic" in God does not stand for a cold, compulsory, inevitable link which binds things together (such a conception has its origin in the fallen world), but rather for a *reasonable* love, a special aspect, that is, of love.

And so it would be true to say in a certain sense that the Logos is the hypostasis of Wisdom, while Wisdom represents the self-determination of the hypostasis of the Logos. Or, to put it more concisely, the Logos in himself is hypostatic Wisdom as such—*kat' exochen* (par excellence). This is a favorite formula on the lips of the opponents of sophiology. Nevertheless, if we want to understand it correctly, its bearing must necessarily be restricted. It can be accepted only in the affirmative, and by no means in a negative or exclusive sense. If we affirm that the Logos *preeminently* represents hypostatic Wisdom, we do not mean to imply that the other hypostases in the Holy Trinity are without Wisdom, and do not possess it at all. Exactly the reverse is true, for Wisdom characterizes all the three Hypostases, each in a special way, exactly as the divine Ousia is shared by all of them. But the Second Hypostasis has the property of being directed immediately toward the Logos, being in this sense identical with the Logos. At the same time the Logos comprises the ideal content of Sophia, so as logically, that is ideally, to determine it.

But Sophia, the Wisdom of God, must also be determined in her relation to the Holy Spirit. To do this, we must recognize as fully as possible the exact hypostatic place of the Holy Spirit within the Holy Trinity. The Third Hypostasis in the Holy Trinity unites the First and the Second Hypostases, the Father with the Son. The Holy Spirit proceeds from the Father to the Son, either "through" (*dia*) the Son, according to the Eastern theologumenon, or through the Father "and" the Son, according to the Western theologumenon.[3] The Holy Spirit "proceeds" from the Father to the Son, as the hypostatic love of the Father, which "abides" in the Son, fulfilling his actuality and possession by the Father. In turn the Holy Spirit passes "through" the Son (*emmesos*),

---

3. For a more extended treatment of the procession of the Holy Spirit, see *The Comforter*, ch. II, pp. 93–186.

returning, as it were, to the Father in a mysterious cycle, as the answering hypostatic love of the Son. In this way the Holy Spirit achieves his own fulfillment as the hypostasis of love. He is Love within love—the Holy Spirit within that tri-hypostatic Spirit which is God.

The Holy Spirit *together with* the Son discloses the Father in the divine Sophia. The Son *and* the Holy Spirit, together, inseparable and unconfused, realize the self-revelation of the Father in his nature. The Son cannot be separated from the Holy Spirit who abides in him; similarly the Holy Spirit is united with the Logos "without confusion." The Ousia being, as Sophia, the self-revelation of the Father within the Holy Trinity must of necessity be concomitantly a revelation of the Logos and of the Holy Spirit.

If we were prepared above to admit conditionally the truth of the formula that in a certain sense the Logos is equivalent to Sophia, we did so only with a particular and limited interpretation in mind. For the Logos, in whom the Holy Spirit abides only in a state of dyadic union (and *not* separated from the tri-unity of the Holy Trinity, to suggest which would be blasphemy!), constitutes Sophia only *with* the Holy Spirit. For this reason the Holy Spirit cannot be separated from Wisdom; he both possesses and reveals her, in inseparable conjunction with the Son. Accordingly in a similar sense we can say that the Holy Spirit too *is* Wisdom, as has in fact been stated by certain Fathers of the Church, such as St. Theophilus of Antioch[4] and St. Irenaeus, Bishop of Lyons.[5]

---

4. Ad. Autolicum 2, 10.
5. Adv. haer. 4, 20.

If the divine Sophia represents a mutual revelation of the Son and of the Holy Spirit, we must try to determine the relationship which exists between them. It is obvious that they neither repeat one another, nor merge together. In spite of this fact, they are mutually identified in *one* self-revelation of the Holy Trinity, in the one Holy Sophia. We find, however, that a very similar statement is made in the trinitarian dogma, which teaches that all the three hypostases—the primary principle, the Father, with the Son and the Holy Spirit—possess one essence and are thereby united in one common life, although as persons they are distinguished. In the same way we should draw the distinction between the two dyadic hypostases in their relation to the divine Sophia.

The hypostasis of the Logos is the only one which completely determines by himself the *content* of Sophia, the ideal *all*, the all-embracing "organism" of ideas, and the ideal unity of them all. There is nothing, nor can anything exist, capable of being added to this or taken from it—even through the Third Hypostasis. Here we should accept as our guiding line the witness of the Incarnate Word about himself and about the Holy Spirit. If in the Old Testament the Holy Spirit is named as "the Spirit of Wisdom," we find that in the New Testament he is described as the "Spirit of Truth" (not, that is, as Wisdom or Truth as such, but precisely as Spirit). "He will guide you into all truth: for he shall not speak of himself; but whatsoever he shall hear, that shall he speak" (John 16.13). "He shall glorify me: for he shall receive of mine, and shall show it unto you. All things that the Father hath are mine: therefore said I, that he shall take of mine, and show it unto you" (14.15). Such is the *transparency* of the Holy Spirit so far as the Son is concerned. By the power of this dyadic union with the Holy Spirit, our Lord promised to send "another Comforter" from the Father, in whose guise, as it were, he comes himself: "I will not leave you comfortless: I will come to you" (John 14.18).

We thus observe that if God's self-revelation in Wisdom is to be defined as far as *content* is concerned as the words of the Word, the divine Word in itself, then the participation of the Holy Spirit in this diune self-revelation relates not to the content, but to the special form and to the divine hypostases in which this content is manifested. The Holy Spirit is the hypostatic love of the Father for the Son, and of the Son for the Father. The revelation of the Son is the divine Thought-Word, the Logos of God concerning himself, "the image and the radiance of the Father," the Thought which contemplates itself and the Word uttering itself. The revelation of the Holy Spirit is accomplished in the existent life of the hypostatic Word, his living actuality for the Father, and thereby for the Holy Spirit himself. It is the hypostatic mutual response of the Father and the Son, their mutually jubilant love, whose exultation is justified by and based upon their mutual sacrificial denial of self, as begetting and begotten. And the Holy Spirit himself constitutes this "perfect joy," the exultation of love between the Father and the Son. The nature of love consists in giving all one possesses without withholding anything for oneself. The one who loves then receives everything for himself or herself only through such a renunciation of self in the beloved. The Holy Spirit as hypostatic love is absolutely transparent in this relationship between the Father and the Son.

In himself he constitutes this transparency, for he is Love. And as such the Holy Spirit represents the principle of the quickening spiritual reality within the Holy Trinity, the reality and the life of the Word of Truth. But the reality of Truth is Beauty, the "good" of Gen. 1.10, 12; the Word becomes adorned by beauty, because the Holy Spirit abides in him. The Holy Spirit who abides in the Son, manifests him to the Father in beauty, for he himself is "the beauty of the Lord" (Ps. 27.4).

In the divine self-revelation, in the Ousia-Sophia, the "Spirit of Wisdom," the Holy Spirit, represents the principle of reality. He transforms the world of ideas into a living and real essence, into a self-sufficient creation of God, the *ens realissimum*, into a world existing with the life of God. This constitutes the divine fiat in God himself in relation to his own being, the content of which is ideally spoken, and is determined, in the Word. But being in God is not, and cannot be, like being in things—a dead objectivity, which incidentally, we only observe in our world because our powers of perception are so limited. No, the world of divine ideas, a world of divine realities, is a living thing, is in fact life itself. And the Holy Spirit is the breath of life, "the breath from the mouth of God."[6]

This *life* of Truth in its own full transparency is *beauty*, which is the self-revelation of the Deity, the garment of God, as it were; it is that divine glory which the heavens declare (Ps. 19.1). It is of this glory, as an aspect of divine manifestation, or epiphany, that Holy Scripture speaks, as

---

6. In the writings of the Fathers of the Church the hypostasis of the Spirit is usually compared with the breath we take when we pronounce a word.

we have seen above. The self-revelation of Wisdom is equivalent to the self-revelation of glory. Wisdom is the glory of God and either expression could be used indiscriminately of divine self-revelation within the Godhead, for they both refer to the same divine essence. Nevertheless we prefer to describe this glory as Sophia the Wisdom of God—in other words to take it as defined in its relationship to the Second Hypostasis, to the Logos, insofar as he gives it *content*, whereas in glory it is defined according to its being. But just as when we consider the mode of the divine self-revelation we must always remember that it is effected conjointly by the Word and the Holy Spirit, so here when we try to define it we must in speaking of Wisdom imply glory also: for Wisdom is the matter of glory, glory the form of Wisdom.

Thus we reach the conception of the self-revelation of the Godhead in the double figure of Wisdom-Glory, which corresponds to the dyad of the Word and of the Spirit. But, it may be said, will not this line of thought lead, as it were, to a splitting up of the one undivided Trinity into two parts: the Father, who alone possesses the divine Wisdom-Glory, and the two revealing hypostases of the Son and of the Holy Spirit, who manifest it in themselves? Are we not introducing in another form the error which we have already refuted: namely that Wisdom in the Holy Trinity can only belong to or be identified with one of the hypostases (as is generally thought, with the second), and *not* be shared by the other hypostases? In other words, is not Wisdom made a basis of division within the Holy Trinity? In answer to which it may be observed that the Ousia is one and undivided in the Holy Trinity and that the Holy Trinity itself, by a triune act, possesses it in common in its one life, and that therefore in a similar way the Ousia-Sophia does not divide the Holy Trinity, but manifests it to itself. The basic postulate of this self-revelation consists in the fact of the fundamental distinction according to which we have the primary hypostasis which is disclosed, the subject of revelation—the Father, who begets the Son and brings forth the Holy Spirit—and also the revealing hypostases, the Son who is begotten of the Father and the Holy Spirit who proceeds from him. The content of this revelation is actually represented by the divine Sophia-Logos, as the manifested image of the divine Ousia. The di-unity of the two revealing hypostases, the dyad of the Son and of the Holy Spirit, manifests the divine Sophia. In this sense we can say that their own self-revelation *is* Sophia. She can therefore be attributed to both the divine hypostases of the Son and of the Spirit, who constitute her diune subject. But at the same time we must retain the truth of the postulate that the dyad of the Son and of the Holy Spirit constitutes the revelation of the Father, so that their self-revelation is at the same time the revelation of the Father himself working in them and through them. Hence Sophia belongs to the Father, for he is her initial and ultimate subject. She represents the disclosure of his transcendence, of the silence and mystery of the Godhead; she is the Father manifesting himself through the Son and the Holy Spirit.

We thus come to the conclusion that the divine Sophia, as the self-revelation of Godhead, belongs to all three persons of the Holy Trinity, both in their tri-unity, and in their separate being, and to each one in a way peculiar to it. She represents their self-revelation, and in this sense, she is their predicate. But we must distinguish between the aspects of this predication. The relation of Sophia to the Second and Third Persons of the Holy Trinity is immediate, insofar as she expresses the image of the hypostatic being of each. The relation of Sophia to the Father is mediated through his relation to the other hypostases, who disclose him to Sophia.

In summing up we can say that the entire Holy Trinity in its tri-unity "is Sophia," just as all the three hypostases are in their separateness. But we should be clear in this connection what we mean by "*is.*" The connecting word "is" here unites the tri-hypostatic subject with the predicate. The subject is a Hypostasis which, according to its nature, possesses being and which discloses this being in its nature. Nevertheless this predicate, as the content of the subject's natural life, does not contain within itself the Hypostasis as such, but only reveals it. And Sophia, in this sense, once more, is *not* a Hypostasis, but only a quality belonging to a Hypostasis, an attribute of hypostatic being. Therefore we should point out a very important peculiarity of such statements as the following: the Father, the Son, the Holy Spirit, or the Holy Trinity "is" either Ousia or Sophia. Such a statement *cannot be reversed.* We cannot on the basis of the foregoing argument affirm the converse in which the place of the subject would be occupied by the Ousia-Sophia, and the place of the predicate by the hypostases, for instance: "Ousia-Sophia is the Father, Son, etc." Such a statement would simply be untrue for it would contain the heresy of impersonalism as regards the Holy Trinity. It would equate with the hypostases a principle which is in itself nonhypostatic although it belongs to the hypostases.

This is the ontological absurdity, the heresy, which characterizes all varieties of impersonal conceptions of the Holy Trinity (beginning with that of St. Augustine, continued in those of Boehme and Eckhart, and culminating in those of Schelling and Hegel).

Thus we have established the relationship which exists between Sophia and the divine Ousia, and at the same time, through this, her relationship to the triune hypostases. Each of these in its specific way possesses Sophia and in this sense is Sophia. The Father, *Deus absconditus* (the hidden God), possesses her as his revelation in the dyad of hypostases which reveals him. The Son possesses her as his own revelation, which is fulfilled, and accomplished through the Holy Spirit. The Holy Trinity possesses her as her triune subject, as it exists in three different hypostases; and in its tri-unity has her as its one Ousia,[7] which in its revelation is the divine Sophia.

---

7. We must here draw attention to the meager interest displayed in the doctrine of the one Ousia in trinitarian theology. This accounts for the absence of sophiology which would otherwise have been evoked by this doctrine. It may even be said that the conception of Ousia has remained in the lifeless scholastic form in which it was taken over from Aristotle. It has merely indicated the *place* where future problems would arise, and had been more of a theological symbol than a theological doctrine. Such a state of things could not last forever, and sophiology has come in our time to occupy this vacant place and reveal the meaning of this symbol.

3

The Divine and
the Creaturely Sophia [1]

The tri-personal God has his own self-revelation. His nature, or Ousia, constitutes his intrinsic Wisdom and Glory alike, which we accordingly unite under the one general term Sophia. God not only *possesses* in Sophia the principle of his self-revelation, but it is this Sophia which *is* his eternal divine life, the sum and unity of all his attributes. And here we must once and for all remove the common scholastic misunderstanding which makes Wisdom no more than a particular "property" or quality, comprised in the definition of God, and therefore devoid of proper subsistence. If this were so, then, since Sophia is Ousia as revealed, the same consequence would follow for Ousia as such. It too would lose its place in the substantial being of the divine Spirit and become no more than a "quality." Such an interpretation

---

1. See my work *The Unfading Light*: the chapters on creation; and *The Lamb of God*, Ch. I: The Divine Sophia, Ch. II: The Creaturely Sophia, pp. 112-169.

obviously materially impairs the dogma of the Holy Trinity. It would imply that God is a Spirit without a nature and that the divine hypostases are in fact devoid of Ousia. Their being would be confined to an abstract relationship of mutual self-abandonment, without any content of nature, a conception akin to the *Ich-Philosophie* of the elder Fichte.[2]

In opposition to this scholastic abstraction which can only lead to heresy regarding the doctrine of the Trinity, we must insist on the full ontological reality of Ousia-Sophia. This is no mere self-determination of the personal God; Ousia, and therefore Sophia, exists for God and in God, as his subsistent divinity. Yet here is no "fourth Hypostasis"; we do not transform the Holy Trinity into a quaternity, but merely recognize precisely in the Ousia the divinity of God, a principle "other" than his hypostases. It is quite natural, of course, for discursive reason to hesitate when confronted with the necessity of drawing a distinction between the hypostatic and the essential, sophianic, being of the one self-sufficient divine Spirit. Such a distinction, however, is only a consequence of the trinitarian dogma, which is a doctrine not only of the hypostases of the Trinity, but also of the consubstantiality of their nature. No more will sound ontology, however, suffer us to reduce the essential nature of the Godhead to the shadowy existence of a logical abstraction.

---

2. We can see a contrary error in the denial of personality in Spirit, leaving it no more than nature devoid of personal consciousness of self. Such is the philosophy of the "unconscious" in Schopenhauer, Hartmann, and Drews.

We are here confronted with an apposition of two postulates, which is for abstract reason an antinomy: 1. God has Ousia or Sophia, in a sense *is* his Ousia or Sophia—that is the thesis of its identity; 2. Ousia or Sophia *exists* only in God, belongs to him, as the very ground of his being—that is the antithesis, distinction. Both affirmations are true: the Ousia or Sophia is the non- hypostatic essence, which yet can exist only in connection with the tri-hypostatic person of God. This antinomy may be somewhat elucidated by comparison with the relationship between spirit and body in human beings. The human spirit cannot exist without the body, any more than the body can exist in isolation from the spirit. As such, the body is not merely an aggregate of bones and muscles belonging to the matter of the world; it is more than mere matter. The body should be understood as a revelation of the spirit, of its likeness and of its life. Being informed by intelligence, it provides the outward expression for human individuality—it is, so to speak, an icon of the spirit which dwells in it. The body, as a living organism, manifests within itself the life of its spirit, and is the spirit's revelation, its creation and its "glory" (cf. Phil. 3.21). The body once separated from the spirit ceases to exist as a body, and becomes a corpse, mere matter: "...for dust thou art and unto dust shalt thou return" (Gen. 3.19); yet equally, once the spirit is separated from the body, the human being, in the fullness of being, no longer exists.

The human being, the incarnate spirit, thus provides us with an obvious example of the antinomy involved in the correlation of hypostatic and non-hypostatic being.

To what extent, then, may this analogy be applied to the mutual relationship between the tri-personal God and his Wisdom? It is usual to define spirit in general, and the divine Spirit in particular, by the negative notion of *incorporeality*, as a being without a body. This is to take for granted that the body is simply the principle directly opposed to spirit. For the purpose of making clearer what the divine Spirit is, we even make use of a comparison with the angels, the bodiless spirits. The incorporeal nature of the angels, however, only marks their special place in creation and their ministry to humanity;[3] in no way can it be taken to express the nature of spirit as such. The angelic world of bodiless spirits should always be thought of in conjunction with the world of human spirits, associated with the body, and by nature revealing itself through this body.

The angels minister to the world of human beings. That is why they are described by contrast, as bodiless beings, a description which at once assigns them a place in the hierarchy of being, and thereby denotes a limitation of their being. No such limitation can be ascribed to the divine Spirit, which has in the Wisdom and Glory identical with its essence the sufficient medium of its self-revelation. On the contrary, it would appear that this self-revelation, described in Scripture under the striking figures of Wisdom and Glory, can with greater truth be compared with or interpreted as the real prototype or exemplar cause of human self-revelation through the body. We know that the Scriptures frequently speak of

---

3. See Bulgakov, *Jacob's Ladder* (on the Angels).

God's "body," or at least of its separate parts or organs: head, ears, eyes, hands, feet, for example. It is usual to interpret this only in the sense of an allegory or an inevitable anthropomorphism. But would it not be more exact to understand it ontologically, in the sense that the organs of the human body, being instruments for revealing the spirit, must themselves have a spiritual prototype in the fullness of the divine life? In other words, the bodily form of the human being corresponds to the formal aspect of that divine Glory, which is itself the fullness of the life of God. Naturally this simile does not hold good when the body has become "flesh" (in the bad sense)—for this state would be more exactly described as a virtual denial of the body—but only so long as the body remains obedient and transparent to the spirit, only so long as it is a "spiritual body" (1 Cor. x15.44). The very expression "spiritual body," far from being a contradiction in terms or a paradox, corresponds to the prime exemplar of the body, which has its prototype in the Wisdom and Glory of God.

Indeed we can pursue this analogy yet further. We can actually draw a distinction within the body between its "reasonable soul" (*psyche noera*) and the sensible body as such, in other words between its form and matter, the principles representative respectively of the Logos and the Spirit, of Reason and of Beauty. Hence the body has a twofold determination, which corresponds to the dyadic character of the self-revelation of God through Wisdom and Glory in the Second and Third Hypostases.

Thus the essential Wisdom and Glory in God possesses an ontological reality analogous to that of a body informed by a reasonable soul in its relation to the spirit incarnate in it. And accordingly it can be compared to an absolute, heavenly, spiritual body belonging to the divine Spirit in all the fullness of its self-revelation. There is reference to this fullness, *pleroma*, in relation to the incarnate Word in the phrase "in him dwelleth all the fullness of the Godhead bodily" (Col. 2.9) That inner self-revelation of God which is described as fullness in reference to his Wisdom and Glory can also be defined as the "world' of God in reference to the personal life of the Deity itself. This life, obviously cannot be without content; on the contrary, it is precisely by its fullness that it tranacends all definition. The simplicity of God's spiritual essence is not mere uniformity any more than the divine unity excludes multiplicity. On the contrary simplicity precisely implies fullness, a fullness in which all qualities meet in one. This unity of all with all and in all is the ground of the energy of love within the Godhead. Sophia, as the "world" of God, represents a "pan-organism" of the ideas of all in the all, while the vital power of this organism is derived from the Holy Spirit. That, in effect, is what the Godhead is for God.

But a question at once arises—can we as creatures presume to penetrate into the inner life of the Deity itself and pronounce any sort of opinion on it? Are not such attempts merely the product of an insane daring and an impotent presumption? Do not the prohibitions of the *via negationis*, the *docta ignorantia*, whose wisdom consists only in knowing that we know nothing, come nearer to the heart of the matter? Such doubts are expressed in various quarters in relation to sophiology. Are they justified?

Now it is true that the absolute God can never be comprehended by human reason. God transcends the world and humankind to such an extent that even the purely negative theology which denies all possibility of knowing anything about God, has nevertheless already gone too far in affirming so much as that. Even negation must make one positive assumption. Indeed, the only thing which seems appropriate is the absence of any sort of thought or teaching about God, a form of agnosticism which merges into practical atheism. God in his mercy, however, has not left us in the darkness of such agnosticism: he has given us a revelation concerning himself. He reveals himself to us both in his tri-personal being and in the simplicity of his deity, and only by virtue of such revelation dare we make any positive statement about God; we not only may, we must.

The absolute god, who exists in himself, self-contained in his absoluteness, self-sufficing in his majesty, abandons this state and establishes in dependence upon his own absolute being a relative creaturely being. It is only in relation to this being that he can be called God.[4] Eternity lays the foundation for time, nonspatial beings for spatial beings, changelessness for becoming, while God abides "in the heavens" in his eternity and absoluteness. This state in which the absoluteness of the Absolute is combined with the relationship joining the world to God, the divine life in itself on the one hand with its manifestation in the created universe on the other, constitutes the ultimate antinomy for our reason and knowledge, a bound

---

4. "The notion of God is a relative one." St. Basil the Great. *Deux est vox relativa.* Sir Isaac Newton.

which we cannot pass. At this point the fiery sword bars the way to our reason, which can do no more than recognize the existence of this antinomy, accepting both its postulates as equally necessary, though by their very essence mutually exclusive. In practice this antinomy can be expressed for us in the following proposition: *the Absolute reveals itself to us as God*; and we learn to know God as such only on the basis of this his revelation of himself in his tri-personal being and in his Godhead, that is, the Glory and Wisdom of his essence.

Alongside the divine and eternal world exists the world of creaturely being established by God in time. And God created it from "nothing." What does this expression mean? It marks in the first place the fact that no other principle of creation exists outside of God or apart from God. This at once excludes that Manichean dualism, according to which side by side with the true God exists some anti-god, who is the true source of the world of creatures. At the same time this affirmation also does away with the pagan materialism which assumes, in such mythological figures as that of Tiamat, the existence of prime matter, as it were, along with God. There can be no source of the world but God. This is as much as to say that the world has been established in its being by God, that it has been created by God by his own power and out of himself. Therefore the creature is distinct from the deity itself not in respect of the source of its being, but only in respect of the particular mode of its reception of that being.

But, meditating on the creation of the world from nothing, we can hardly help asking ourselves whether this "nothing" existed "before" creation and, as it were, on the other side of creation. We cannot imagine this "nothing" as in any way forming a limitation for God, nor can we think of it as a void, somehow "surrounding" God's being. "Nothing" means "no thing," not "a thing" existing outside God. Hence, in order to *be*, "nothing" itself must originate in, must be established by God, who, according to an expression of Pseudo-Dionysius is (in this sense) the creator even of "nothing." Indeed, non-being is itself a symptom or manifestation of the presence of being. In a certain sense the two are dialectically identifiable, as, for example, they are identified in Plato's *Parmenides*. "Nothing" here merely expresses the character of created being, with its relativity, incompleteness, *becoming*. Every such form of being must necessarily find its origin outside itself. Its emergence represents the filling of a void, of some deficiency of being, by some more positive, though still incomplete, form of being. In this process of filling in, the non-being, the "nothing," itself acquires as it were a title to existence. In the act of emergence two poles are present: the positive source of being and the void of non-being, which is being replenished by its fullness. And in this sense fullness alone truly *exists*, while "nothing" is but the counterpart of this fullness in the state of deficiency. It is being in the process of becoming. Creatureliness as such consists in this fusion of being and nothingness, or of being and non-being. The process of becoming lies at the very root of creatureliness—of its lack of power to gain existence for itself, its dependence on the bestowal of that power from above, in which consists the fact of creation. This is the manifestation outside God of the wealth of divine being, now enshrined in creation and existing in dependence upon the divine being.

If, then, the world does not possess in itself the capacity to exist, but acquires it from God, we may well inquire, what is the relation between the divine power sustaining the being of the world and God's own inner life, his nature—Wisdom?

The first and most fundamental question is this: is the content of the life of the world, or rather are the divine principles on which it is based, something new for God himself, which was unknown to him prior to creation and which was lacking in him, apart from his relationship to creation? To raise this question it is enough to be able to see the obvious answer. For as soon as we admit that the principle of creation is something *new* to God himself, we must recognize a certain incompleteness in God without creation. This inevitably forces us to the further conclusion that the creation of the world is, in some sense, a sort of self-revelation for God himself. Let us make this assumption that with creation something new emerges in God, which did not exist before. But this in its turn cuts at the very roots of God's absoluteness and self-sufficiency, and denies the fullness of divine life within him. We see, therefore, that such an affirmation leads to the theological absurdity and contradiction that the self-sufficient God creates the world in response to a certain need for fulfillment, and in the world discovers something new to himself.

It is obviously, then, essential for us to accept the opposite point of view. God creates the world, as it were, out of himself, out of the abundance of his own resources. Nothing new is introduced for God by the life of the world of creatures. That world only receives, according to the mode proper to it, the divine principle of life. Its being is only a reflection and a mirror of the world of God. We find this line of thought in the teaching of some of the Fathers of the Church. For them, God contained within himself before the creation of the world the divine prototypes, *paradeigmata*, the destinies, *proörismoi*, of all creatures, so that the world bears within it the image and, as it were, the reflection of the divine prototype. We find such teaching even in those Fathers of the Church who in dealing with the subject of Wisdom, especially in their interpretation of Prov. 8.22, remained under the influence of the difficulties raised by Arius, and were thus apt to identify Wisdom simply with the hypostasis of the Son. Yet in spite of this, in their teaching on the creation of the world they affirm the existence of the divine prototypes of creation, in full accordance with the sophiological point of view. Such, for example, is the teaching of St. Athanasius.[5] The Pseudo-Dionysius quite definitely speaks of such prototypes,[6] as do St. John of Damascus,[7] St. Maximus the Confessor and St. Gregory of Nyssa, St. Augustine,[8] and,

---

5. See Bulgakov, *The Burning Bush*, excursus III.

6. De divin. nom. c. 5, IX. Migne. Patr. Gr. t. 3, c. 824: "The prototypes exist in God as essential and complete (*heviaios*) pre-existent bases, which are described by theology as predestinations (*proörismous*)."

7. *In Defence of the Holy Icons against Gainsayers*: I, X; III, XIX. "The second aspect of the image is the thought which exists in God in regard to that which he is to create, his eternal counsel, which is ever the same, *for the Deity is immutable, and its counsel has no beginning....* For images and examples of all that shall be created by God are simply his thought in him of these objects. . .in his counsel we see traced out and represented what he has foreordained; this is his thought of each such object."

8. Ang Tr. I. in Joan. Migne. Patr. Lat. t. 34-35. c. 1387.

perhaps with the greatest precision and directness, St. Gregory Nazianzen.[9]

What then are these eternal prototypes of creation, which are recognized by the Fathers of the Church as its divine foundation? Although the Fathers themselves do not describe them by the name of the divine Sophia, nevertheless in essence we have here, quite undoubtedly, the divine world considered as the prototype of the creaturely. Thus the doctrine of Sophia as the prototype of creation finds ample support in the tradition of the Church. If in the light of what has been stated above we turn to Prov. 8.22–23, and the parallels in the pseudepigrapha (see above ch. I) it will not be difficult for us to convince ourselves that here also the Wisdom of God is represented precisely as a prototype of creation existing with God prior to the creation of the world. It is the delight in creation of God the "cunning workman."

---

9. Carmina Mystica. Mign. Patr. Gr. t. 37, c. 472.

> "I ask: If to God we can never ascribe either inactivity or incompleteness, then whereupon was the supreme mind engaged during that all eternity wherein he reigned over the void, while as yet he had not made the world, and adorned it with forms?
>
> The object of his contemplation then was the adorable radiance of his own goodness and intelligence, and the equal perfection of glory of all the thrice-radiant Godhead, no less truly so to himself in his solitude than to those unto whom he has now revealed it. *And likewise that mind whence the world is begotten then dwelt in the depth of his mind upon how he should give shape to that world which was afterward brought into being, and which even then was thus present to God.*
>
> For God has all things ever under his eye, both what is yet to be, and what was, and is now. The division whereby one thing is before another or after in time is imposed upon me; but for God all is fused into one, and held in the grasp of his Godhead."

"And Wisdom was with thee: which knoweth thy works, and was present when thou madest the world" (Wisdom of Sol. 9.9). When God made the world "then did he see it and declare it [Wisdom]" (Job 28.27).

However we may in other respects interpret the biblical teaching on Wisdom in relation to the divine hypostases, there is no doubt that it includes this doctrine of the divine prototypes of creation in God: by Wisdom God made the world (cf. Ps. 104.24). Usually these ideas are rationalistically interpreted in the sense that God created the world *wisely*, as if Wisdom were no more than an attribute of God. The inadequacy of such an interpretation is, however, obvious. Wisdom is to be understood ontologically, not as an abstract quality, but as the ever-present power of God, the divine essence, as the Godhead itself. The former way of interpreting such passages as Prov. 8.22–31 was determined by the fact that Wisdom was simply equated with the hypostatic Logos, the creator of the world, through whom "all things were made; and without him was not anything made that was made" (John 1.3; cf. Rom. 2.36). Such an interpretation, however, proves too much, in effect making the Logos alone of the Holy Trinity the creator of the world. This is to contradict the irrefragable fact that the creation of the world was the work of the whole Holy Trinity. But, further, the usual formula used by the Fathers appropriates the creation of the world to the Father, working *through* the Word *by* the Holy Spirit, attributing to the latter an almost instrumental role. They are even compared to God's hands in the work of creation by St. Basil the Great among others.[10]

In what is revealed about creation it is emphasized that it has a "beginning." "In the beginning God created the heaven and the earth" (Gen. 1.1), "The Lord possessed me in the beginning of his way" (Prov. 8.22). To this it is natural to add John 1.1: "In the beginning was the Word." It is usual to interpret this "beginning" as a matter of temporal succession and to see no more in it than an indication of the order or sequence of events. This is especially strange in relation to John 1.1. If what has been argued above holds good, this "beginning" imports rather a divine principle of life, the essential Wisdom of God. If we adopt this interpretation, then all these texts become evidence for a principle in God which gives rise to the world: God created the world by his divinity, by that Wisdom whereby he eternally reveals himself unto himself. It is for this reason that the same revelation (John 1.1) includes the Word and the Holy Spirit.

In general, our position here is to maintain that God in his three persons created the world on the *foundation* of the Wisdom common to the whole Trinity. This is the meaning which underlies the narrative of the creation of the world in six days (Gen. 1.3-31). We have then the following general scheme of creation: God creates by his Word, calling all things into existence by his creative *fiat*,

---

10. St. Basil describes the Father as initiating (*prokatarktike*), the Son as sustaining (*demourgike*), the Holy Spirit as crowning (*teleistike*) the work of creation. St. John of Damascus speaks of the Father as the source and author of creation, the Son as the power of the Father predisposing creation, and the Holy Ghost as fulfilling all—"The Father did all by the Word, as it were by his hand, and creates nothing without him." Cf. also: "The Word is God's will." Athan. Contra Arianos. II.

"God said. . . ." We can distinguish here the person of the Creator—God the Father, "The Father Almighty, maker of heaven and earth and of all things visible and invisible"; his creative Word; and its accomplishment. Certainly, the Word, which contains in itself every word of God concerning creation, and the Spirit, who brings all to fulfillment, are equally persons in the Holy Trinity. It is quite obvious, however, from the text, that it is precisely the Father in person who initiates this act of God, while the Son and the Holy Spirit participate in creation only in virtue of their self-determination in Sophia, the words of the Word and the fulfillment of the Spirit. It is not the Word itself which speaks the creative word, but "God"—the Father[11]—who affirms it by his command "Let there be. . . ." Although the tri-personal God creates the world with each person participating in accordance with its personal character, nevertheless, the very manner of this participation is differently determined for the different persons of the Holy Trinity. In creation the Father alone acts "hypostatically" in the name of God, while the Son and the Spirit abandon themselves to the will of the Father as his word and action. It is the Father who speaks and not the Son, though the words are those of the Word, as it is the Father who creates and not the Spirit, though the Spirit's is the quickening power. Son and Spirit participate in creation not hypostatically so

---

11. This non-hypostatic, sophianic character of the participation of the Second and Third Hypostases in the creation of the world by the Father is indirectly supported by the fact that, as distinct from the rest of creation, the human being as a hypostatic spirit is created sharing in the likeness of all three persons of the Holy Trinity. This is clear from the plural used: "Let *us* make man in *our* image, after our likeness" (Gen. 1.26).

much as sophianically, revealing themselves in Wisdom. So it is said of the Son, "All things were made by him; and without him was not anything made that was made" (John 1.3), and of the Holy Spirit that by the breath of the Father's mouth the strength of the heavens is established (Ps. 33.6; and 104.30 in the Slavonic version).

We can, therefore, say that God the Father creates the world by Sophia,[12] which is the revelation of the Son and of the Holy Spirit. At the same time we should bear in mind that Sophia does not exist in God independently of the divine hypostases, but is eternally hypostatized in them. Yet it is quite possible to draw a distinction within the self-revelation of the Godhead to the effect that this self-revelation may be predominantly determined by reference either to the hypostases, or to Sophia. In the one case we have a revelation predominantly hypostatic, in the other sophianic. So the creation of the world displays the following relationship: the hypostatic Creator is the Father, who, being the principle of procession in the Holy Trinity, creates the world by an act of the whole Trinity in its unique wisdom. In this act the Second and Third Hypostases participate not as separate persons, but somehow "kenotically," concealing themselves in the hypostasis of the Father, from whom initiates the will to create.

The divine Sophia, as the revelation of the Logos, is the *all-embracing unity*, which contains within itself all the fullness of the world of ideas. But to the creature also, God the Creator entrusts this *all*, withholding nothing in himself and not limiting the creature in any way: "All

---

12. See Bulgakov, *The Comforter.*

things were made by him [the Word]" (John 1.3). In Sophia the fullness of the ideal forms contained in the Word is reflected in creation. This means that the species of created beings do not represent some new type of forms, devised by God, so to speak, *ad hoc*, but that they are based upon eternal, divine prototypes.[13] For this reason therefore the world of creatures also bears a "certain imprint"[14] of the world of God, insofar as it shares the fullness of the divine forms or ideas. This is clear from the fact that on accomplishing the work of creation God "rested from all his work" (Gen. 2.1–3). This similitude implies the exhaustive fullness of creation, whose twofold aspect as the creation of both "heaven and earth," the world of angels and the world of humans, does not affect the general postulate that the primary foundation of the world is rooted in divine Sophia.

God bestowed on the world at its creation not only the fullness of its ideal form as present to his own mind, but also the capacity to maintain its own distinct existence. This is the life which it derives from the Holy Spirit. "When thou lettest thy breath go forth, they shall be made. When thou takest away their breath, they die" (Ps. 104.29, 30). The action of the Holy Spirit consists in the direct or indirect application of the creative *fiat* to the different aspects of creation: "Let the waters, let the

---

13. The Platonic doctrine of ideas represents one philosophical form of sophiology, which, however, finds no support in the revelation of the tripersonal God. Cf. *The Unfading Light* .

14. According to his favorite expression, St. Athanasius compares the relationship between the created and the divine Wisdom (which in a one-sided manner he identifies only with the Logos) with "the tracing of the name of the King's son on every building of the town which his Father builds" (Contra Ar. II, 49).

earth, bring forth..." (Gen. 1.20, 24). The quickening activity of the Holy Spirit bestows on creatures in general the capacity to exist, prior to the emergence of their specific forms: "The Spirit of God moved upon the face of the waters" (Gen. 1.2), that is to say, over prime matter, communicating the capacity for existence to the *tohu-bohu* of the "void." The Holy Spirit, who thus imparts to ideal forms their reality, represents the power of *Beauty* or the divine Glory. The Father confers glory on creation after the likeness of divine Glory. The divine approval of creation is repeated as a sort of ratification of the work of each "day"—starting with the third: "and God saw that it was good" (Gen. 1.10, 12, 18, 21, 25). This culminates in the general approbation of everything created. "And God saw everything that he had made and, behold, it was very good" (5.31). "His work is worthy to be praised and had in honor" (Ps. 111.3). This the Slavonic renders, "His work is glory and beauty."

Thus God created the world by the Word and by the Holy Spirit, as they are manifested in Wisdom. In this sense he created the world by Wisdom and after the image of Wisdom. That Wisdom, which is an eternal reality in God, also provides the foundation for the existence of the world of creatures. Once again here we may repeat the dogmatic assertion that the world is created out of "non-being" or "nothing." Yet its capacity to exist, and its abiding reality, is not without some ground. This it finds precisely in the Wisdom of God. To admit this is to affirm, in a sense, the fundamentally divine character of the world, based upon this identity of the principle of divine Wisdom in God and in the creature. Wisdom in creation is ontologically identical with its prototype, the same Wisdom that exists in God. The world exists in God: "For of him, and through him, and to him, are all things" (Rom. 2.36). It exists by the power of his Godhead, even though it exists outside God. It is here that we find the boundary which separates Christianity from any kind of pantheism. In the latter the world is identical with God, and, therefore, strictly speaking neither the world nor God exists, but only a world which is a god in process of becoming. In the Christian conception on the other hand, the world belongs to God, for it is in God that it finds the foundation of its reality. Nothing can exist outside God, as alien or exterior to him. Nevertheless, the world, having been created from "nothing," in this "nothing" finds its "place." God confers on a principle which originates in himself an existence distinct from his own. This is not pantheism, but panentheism.

The created world, then, is none other than the creaturely Sophia, a principle of relative being, in process of becoming, and in composition with the non-being of "nothing"; this is what it means when we say that *the world is created by God from nothing.* Nevertheless, though the positive principle on which the world is based belongs to the being of God, the world as such maintains its existence and its identity distinct from that of God. Although its whole being depends upon the divine power of the creaturely Sophia within it, nevertheless the world is not God, but only God's creature. There is no such ontological necessity for the world that could constrain God himself to create it for the sake of his own development or fulfillment; such an idea would indeed be pure pantheism. On the contrary, God creates the world in the freedom of his superabundant love. The self-sufficiency of God's being is completely realized in the tri-hypostatic life of the consubstantial Deity; nothing else can add to it or give it further fulfillment. In this sense, that is, for his own sake, God does not need the world.

Nevertheless the divine freedom which has manifested itself in the creation of the world is not something haphazard, nor some casual whim of such a kind that the world might equally well have been created or not. The reason for its creation is to be found in a quite different, free "necessity"—the force of God's love overflowing beyond the limits of its own being to found being other than his own. In any other view God's absoluteness would set a limit to the Absolute itself. In the creation of the world any such limitation is transcended by God's omnipotence. Through the act of creation the Absolute descends into the relative. That which does not exist is brought into being by the omnipotence of the Absolute, who is in fact the God who is Love. The Absolute then abides not only within its own absoluteness, but also outside itself, so that the world finds a God in it. This diffusion of God's love into creation is accomplished not in virtue of any *natural* necessity (as Plotinus, for example, thought). It is a *personal* creative act of God, his voluntary self-abandonment in love *ad extra.* But in creating the world by his omnipotence from "nothing" God communicates to it something of the vigor of his own being, and, in the divine Sophia, unites the world with his own divine life. Insofar as the creature is able to bear it, God communicates Sophia, the creaturely Sophia, to creation.

Already as far back as the time of Philo, and later during the Arian controversies, the question had arisen of the need for some mediating principle between God and the world.[15] This problem remained unsolved during the period of christological controversy. The necessity of some such mediation cannot be denied, wherever the distinction of the world from God is held together with its participation in his being. Nevertheless the hypostasis of the Logos cannot provide such a unifying principle between God and the world. This assumption inevitably led to the subordinationism evident in the Christology of Tertullian and Origen, and, more particularly, of Arius. The principle we require is not to be sought in the person of God at all, but in his Nature, considered first as his intimate self-revelation, and second as his revelation in the world. And here we have at once Sophia in both its aspects, divine and creaturely. Sophia unites God with the world as the one common principle, the divine ground of creaturely existence. Remaining one, Sophia exists in two modes, eternal and temporal, divine and creaturely. It is of the first importance for us to grasp both the unity and the "otherness" in this unique relation of the creature to its Creator.

The act of creation itself remains a mystery to the creature. It is a mystery which goes deeper than the being of the creature, to the production of existence from non-existence through the omnipotence of God. Neverthe-

---

15. It was to meet this difficulty that St. Athanasius produced his doctrine of the two aspects of Wisdom, the divine and the created. He develops it in his polemic against the Arians, in particular in his exegesis of Prov. 8.22. See Bulgakov, *The Burning Bush*, excursus III.

less we can dimly discern the limitations of created being, since we come upon them in our inward and outward experience inasmuch as we ourselves belong to this world of creatures.[16] The fundamental mark of the created world is becoming,[17] emergence, development, fulfillment. As a process this involves succession, variety, limitations of space, restriction—all these are aspects of being in the state of becoming. But although this becoming constitutes development, it does not represent evolution from nothing, in the way that this is usually interpreted in theories of evolution, for *ex nihilo nihil fit.* On the contrary, this development represents the germination of the divine seeds of being in the soil of nonbeing, the actualization of divine prototypes, of the divine Sophia in the creaturely. Nevertheless the seed remains only a seed, and not the plant itself. The world of becoming must travel by the long road of the history of the universe if it is ultimately to succeed in reflecting in itself the face of the divine Sophia, and be "transfigured" into it. The creaturely Sophia, which is the foundation of the being of the world, its entelechy, *entelecheia* (in Aristotelian language), is at present in a state of potentiality, *dynamis,* while at the same time it is the principle of its actualization and finality. The world is created in all its fullness, and God "rested from his works" after creation. This fullness, however, only applies to the content of the world as God intended it to be when he created it; it is not true of the present state of the world. The world

---

16. See Bulgakov, *The Unfading Light,* the chapters on creatureliness.
17. Vladimir Solovyov in this sense describes the world as "the Absolute in the state of becoming."

created from nothing both is, and at the same time is not, the creaturely likeness of divine Sophia; it only approximates to this likeness in the course of the world process.

It is possible to ask: Is not the creation of the world, as it were, a sort of duplication of the divine Sophia? But the whole conception of correspondence is inapplicable to the relation between the eternal and becoming. Indeed, it is nearer the truth to speak of unity, even identity, as between the divine and the creaturely Sophia, for nothing is doubled in God. At the same time, however, and without equivocation, we can speak of the two different forms of Sophia in God and in the creature. They are distinguished, on the one hand, as the simple and simultaneous perfection of eternity, as against temporal becoming, and, on the other, as divine, as against participated being. The identity and distinction, the unity and duality of Sophia in God and in creation, rest on the same foundation.

This *coincidentia oppositorum* finds its expression on this account in a relation of type and antitype, an identity in distinction, and distinction in identity. This is the primary and ultimate antinomy of sophiology. And this sophiological antinomy only serves to express the still deeper antinomy from which all theological thought springs and to which it inevitably returns: that of the identity and distinction of God and the Absolute. Absolute being, self-existent and self-sufficing, while maintaining all its absolute character, yet establishes as it were alongside or outside of itself a state of relative being, to which it stands as God. The Absolute is God, but God is not the Absolute insofar as the world relates to him. We find this theological antinomy reflected in a whole series of paradoxical relationships: God and the world, the divine and the creaturely Sophia, the type and the anti-type.[18]

We must now take the last step in our endeavor to define the relationship between type and prototype, between the creaturely and the divine Sophia. The created world belongs to humanity.[19] Humanity, created on the sixth day to have dominion over the world (Gen. 1.26-27), is not merely one among other creatures; it is the representative of all creation, including in itself all the fullness, a microcosm, a world in little, according to the expression of the Fathers. Even the angels, the incorporeal world, minister to humanity and, insofar as they participate in this human world, are dependent on it. In this sense we may say the world is humanity, which includes in itself the formality of all the rest. And for this reason too, God's image in creation is the human form. This also

---

18. See Bulgakov, *The Unfading Light,* the chapters dealing with positive and negative theology. In order to avoid misconceptions let us remind the reader that an antinomy differs both from a logical and a dialectical contradiction. An antinomy simultaneously admits the truth of two contradictory, logically incompatible, but ontologically equally necessary assertions. An antinomy testifies to the existence of a mystery beyond which the human reason cannot penetrate. This mystery, nevertheless, is actualized and lived in religious experience. All fundamental dogmatic definitions are of this nature. It is futile to attempt to dispel or to remove an antinomy. In a logical contradiction, however, exactly the opposite is the case. Such a contradiction is always an indication of a mistake in reasoning which should be detected and removed. Hegel's "dialectic" contradiction, for instance, is in no sense an antinomy. It only applies to discursive reason, which is incapable of embracing contradictory propositions, but retains all its rights in the order of logic, where dialectic is the means of advance.
19. See Bulgakov, *The Lamb of God,* ch. I, 4; II, 3-4; *The Comforter,* ch. IV, a, b.

agrees with the basic fact that humanity was created in *God's image* (Gen. 1.27). We should accept this revelation in its full force and significance.[20] This "image" is the *ens realissimum* in humanity, it establishes a true identity between the image and its prototype, which involves not only the "divinity" of humanity on account of the image of God in it, but also a certain "humanity" of God. As St. Paul puts it, "We are the offspring of God" (Acts 17.28).

In the vision of Glory beheld by the prophet Ezekiel we find the following significant passage: "And above the firmament that was over their heads was the likeness of a throne, as the appearance of a sapphire stone: and upon the likeness of the throne was a likeness as the appearance of a *man* upon it above" (1.26). This is precisely the similitude of heavenly humanity. We come across the same human image of God in Daniel's vision (7.9–13): "And behold, there came with the clouds of heaven one like unto a Son of Man, and he came even to the ancient of days and they brought him near before him."[21]. The New Testament likewise speaks of the heavenly human being, chiefly in relation to Christ: "He that descended

---

20. In patristic writings we find the greatest measure of such an acceptance in St. John of Damascus (*In Defence of the Holy Icons*, III, XVII-XX): "Every image is a revelation of knowledge concerning what lies hidden.... The first, natural, and unchangeable image of the invisible God is the Son of the Father.... And the Holy Spirit—the image of the Son.... The second type of image is God's thought of what he was about to create, his eternal counsel.... The third type of image is that which God created himself in his own likeness, to wit, man." (Migne, Patr. Gr. t. 96, 1339-4I.)

21. Instances of angels appearing in human form, which are at the same time theophanies, would also be applicable here. A very important example is that of the three men who appeared to Abraham, in which many see a manifestation of the Holy Trinity: cf. Rublev's celebrated icon.

out of heaven, even the Son of Man" (John 3.13). "The first man is of the earth, earthy; the second man is of heaven" (1. Cor. 15.47). "The gift of grace of the one man, Jesus Christ" (Rom. 5.15). The Incarnation is closely connected with this heavenly or eternal humanity. There is something in human beings which is directly related to the essence of God. It is no one natural quality, but our whole humanity, which is the image of God. It has its own line of development, its own history, but it is already fixed and marked out in human beings, as a constant tendency at the very heart of our being. It lies within us, something as yet unrevealed, yet surely to be revealed, if only when "God shall be all in all" (1 Cor. 15.28).

Divine Sophia as humanity, or rather as a principle within humanity, is not as yet identical with humanity. For the human being is a hypostasis, in which alone humanity, human nature, exists. Thus Sophia in itself does not as yet express the whole of humanity, which necessarily requires a hypostasis. Human beings receive this at the time of their creation by the breath of the spirit of God. This is their Ego, in which, and through which alone, their humanity lives. But human nature already has the capacity for receiving a hypostasis, after the likeness of its prototype, the divine Sophia, which can never exist without a hypostasis, but is eternally hypostatized. The hypostasis of the Logos is (in the special sense mentioned above) that proper to the divine Sophia. We can say of the Logos that he is the everlasting human being, the human prototype, as well as the Lamb slain "before the foundation of the world"—in other words, predestined to become the representative human being on earth. The

Third Hypostasis does not in this way form a hypostatic center for heavenly humankind, Divine-humanity, as a reality in God, to the Son, and through him to the Father also. In this sense we can distinguish within the eternal Divine-humanity the Logos as the God-human, and the Holy Spirit, as its divine humanity. In consequence there is a difference in the relationship between the Logos and Divine-humanity and that between the Holy Spirit and Divine-humanity. But the Son and the Holy Spirit together[22] constitute Divine-humanity, as the revelation of the Father in the Holy Trinity. The nature of this relationship between the Second and Third Hypostases in regard to Divine-humanity, can also be considered as that of those principles in the Godhead, which in creaturely humankind are reflected in the relation between masculinity and femininity. God's image in humankind is not fully unfolded without the interrelation of these two principles (Gen. 1.27).

This same relation, since the Incarnation, is reflected in that between Christ and the Church. Human hypostases are reflections of the Logos, the Heavenly Human, the "new Adam." But the Holy Spirit, since it abides in the Son, is also a prototype of human hypostases. Thus human beings, created in the image of God, have been created male and female. Husband and wife, though they differ as two different exemplifications of human nature, manifest in their unity the fullness of humanity and of the image of God enshrined in it. Their union is sealed by the dyad of the Son and of the Holy

---

22. See Bulgakov *The Comforter*, the chapters on the dyad of the Son and the Holy Spirit; similarly the epilogue *The Father*.

Spirit, which reveals the Father. They bear within themselves the power of procreation, the image of the unity of the tri-personal God, which is to be traced in the whole of humankind as such.

Finally, the image of God, enshrined in human beings, is inseparably bound up with his *likeness*. The two are related to each other as something *given*, implanted by God, and something *imposed* upon humans, the task they are called upon to fulfil in their creative freedom. The realization of this task is a painful process, full of temptations and demanding effort, but at the same time it is the royal road, an effort wherein the human being can imitate God. Nevertheless for limited creaturely being, temptation is always possible. Hence Adam's fall and what is called Original Sin. But even in their fall human beings cannot destroy the image of God within them; it is only obscured. However, as soon as humanity fell, the whole of created nature also fell into disorder, for it was all bound up with humanity. And the reinstatement of fallen humanity takes place only in Divine-humanity, in the incarnation of the Word and the outpouring of the Holy Spirit.

4

The Incarnation [1]

There is plain evidence of Scripture for the opinion that the descent of Christ into the world at his Incarnation was included in God's eternal counsel concerning the world, "ordained before the foundation of the world." Christ is "the lamb without blemish and without spot: foreordained before the foundation of the world, but manifest in these last times" for us (1 Peter 1.20; cf. 1 Cor. 2.7; Eph. 1, 4-6, 9-10; 3.9-11). The love of God did not stop short at the creation of the world, but determined his own descent into it in person. In view of the Fall, the Incarnation, as it in fact took place, was obviously primarily an atonement. But its purpose extends beyond this to the complete divinization of the creation, and the union of things in heaven and things on earth under the headship of Christ.

---

1. Cf. Bulgakov, *The Lamb of God.* The sophiological Christology here exposed only in outline is there systematically developed.

What then is the ground of the Incarnation? Is it an act of divine omnipotence, comparable to the creation of the world *ex nihilo?* Or does not the fact of the Incarnation itself suppose the presence in human nature of some inalienable characteristic which makes the possibility of the Incarnation comprehensible, not as the invasion of human nature by some *deus ex machina,* but, on the contrary, as the complete unfolding of its possibilities? Evidently the latter explanation is preferable. The possibility of the Word being made human underlies the very creation of humankind, which seems in consequence to make ready to receive him.

In its creation humanity receives a wordless call to reach heaven. That is the task set before it, which, however, it cannot perform with its own strength, but only in the power of God. In view of the fact of the Fall, this aspiration towardsunion with God took the form of the prophetic prediction of Emmanuel, the Redeemer (Job 19.25–27). For this purpose it seems natural that the Person sent by the Father into the world to become incarnate should be that of the Son; for the Word is the prototype *par excellence* of humankind (see above). The person who actually effects the incarnation of the Word, however, appears to be the Holy Ghost, sent down upon the Virgin Mary.

Only as the result of centuries of dogmatic development did the Church, in the Fourth General Council at Chalcedon, produce the fundamental dogma of the God-human and Divine-humanity; though the latter expression is not, as a matter of fact, employed in the definition. According to this definition, there is in Christ but one person, existing in two natures, the divine and the human, and that this is the Second Person of the Holy Trinity, the Word. It was long before theological thought could hit upon the distinction finally attained in this definition. Christological controversy found expression in the acute differences between the school of Alexandria and that of Antioch; on the one hand, the monophysites confused the two natures, supposing the human absorbed by the divine; on the other, the diphysites dissolved them, dividing the one God-human into two persons. The solution sought for was found at Chalcedon, in this unity of person within the duality of natures, in the form not of a theological synthesis, but simply of a dogmatic definition affirming thesis and antithesis together.

This fact gives particular prominence to one feature of the dogma. The relation of the two natures in Christ is there defined not positively, but in a series of negations— *inconfuse, immutabiliter, indivise, inseparabiliter* (unconfusedly, immutably, indivisibly, inseparably)—so that *salva proprietate utriusque, naturae. . .in unam personam atque substantiam concurrent* (without detriment to the "ownness" of each [individuality/uniqueness] , the[ir] natures will converge in[to] one person and substance). For all its great and fundamental significance for Christian faith, this definition undeniably confronts theological thought with fresh difficulties. It is, in fact, thereby invited to go beyond the negations of Chalcedon to the affirmations there tacitly assumed. In other words, a proper comprehension of the definition demands a whole series of dogmatic postulates, which we must now expose.

According to the definition, Christ, being "One altogether," perfect "as touching his Godhead" and "as touching his Manhood," existing as one person in two natures, lives in both and, of course, with but a single life. Moreover the humanity of the God-human is "enhypostatic" (*enhypostos*) as Leontius of Byzantium expressed it, in the Word. That is, the divine person of the Word became that of a human nature as well. The suggestion was subsequently taken to be metaphysically possible, and sufficiently established. But how is it possible? On what is it established? Can human nature receive and make room for the divine person of the Word together with, or, more precisely, in the stead of the human person? What does this imply?

Human nature is elsewhere to be found only in the possession of a human person, and seems to admit of no other owner. From this we must infer that, since the person of the Word found it possible to live in human nature as well as in its own, therefore it is itself in some sense a human person too. It must be somehow co-natural not only with God, but also with the human, that is, with the God-human. In order to serve as a person to humanity, the divine person of the Word must itself be human or, more exactly, "co-human." Its union with human nature will then not appear to do violence to the latter, dissolving or annihilating it, but to correspond to the original relation between them. Humankind, on its side, must be naturally capable of receiving and making room for a divine person in the stead of the human. In other words, the human being's original mode of being is theandric.

The Incarnation thus appears to postulate, on its hypostatic side at least, some original analogy between divine and human personality, which yet does not overthrow all the essential difference between them. And this is found in the relation between type and prototype. The personal spirit of the human being has its divine, uncreated origin from "the spirit of God" (Gen. 2.7). It is a spark of the divine. Through this spirit, humanity is indeed made a partaker in the divine nature, and seen to be capable of divinization. This spirit once united with and animating a human nature "of a reasonable soul, and human flesh subsisting," the human being already appears, by composition and destiny alike, to be, in a true sense, theandric. And though humanity's present state of sin obscures our memory of our heavenly birth, yet we have something in us which asks for Divine-humanity. Even before his coming the Christ who was to be was somehow contained in humankind. But humankind itself has no power to bring to pass the new birth in the spirit, which is "not of blood nor of the will of the flesh, but of God."

If the human being, the creature, is by destiny thus theandric, the Word, on the other hand, who is the prototype, is the everlasting God-human. It is in this sense that we take the position which lies at the base of all St. Paul's teaching on the human being. He speaks not of one, but of two: "The first man is of the earth, earthy: the second man is the Lord from heaven" (1 Cor. 15.47–49; John 3.3), the "one man Jesus Christ" (Rom. 5.15). Thus it was possible for the person of the heavenly God-human, the Word, to become the person of a created human nature, and so realize its original Divine-humanity. Since from all eternity the person of the Word was somehow human, it was possible for it, in becoming the person of a created human nature, to elevate that nature without destroying it. We may even say that it was "natural" for the Word to take the place of the human personality of the human nature of Christ. And this is evidently possible because human personality in general is itself supernatural, and stands for the divine principle in the human makeup. So the Word provides the person for the humanity of Christ also in his character as the second Adam. So, too, it was possible for human nature in Christ to receive and assume a divine person in the quality of its own personality. And so we confess Christ to be perfect God and perfect human being, and the human compound in him to be maintained entire, for there is sufficient metaphysical ground for the possibility of the Word's descent into humanity. That spirit which in human beings is human, though derived from God, in Christ is the everlasting Word, the Spirit of God, the Second Person of the Holy Trinity.

The Word, in assuming an animated body, assumes the whole nature of the human being—s*arx* (flesh), St. Paul's equivalent for the phrase of the Council's *ek Psyches noeras kai somatos*—while maintaining his divine nature in indissoluble union with his person. What does this duality of natures in a single person here import? In the Chalcedonian definition their relation is defined only in negative terms: "inseparably and unconfusedly." But there must be some positive relation between them.[2]

The union of the two natures, the divine and the human, must be something more than the mere mechanical conjunction of two alien principles. That

---

2. In explication of this definition the Sixth General Council affirmed the existence in Christ of two parallel and concordant wills and energies, and thereby gave a less abstract idea of this positive relation.

would be a metaphysical impossibility. And it would be wrong to call in divine omnipotence to justify what is contrary to nature as established by God himself in creating it. The omnipotence of God concerns the original creation of the world. In his providential government of it he maintains inviolate the nature which he gave it. The real basis of the union of the two natures in Christ seems to lie in their mutual relationship as two variant forms of divine and created Wisdom. It is conceivable only because humanity is the created form of divine Wisdom, which is simply God's nature revealing itself.

Consequently, along with the distinction between the two natures of Christ, an analogy of being is established. Here, in fact, we have the affirmation implicitly contained in the negations of Chalcedon. Apart from this analogy, the union of natures would be just such a metaphysical absurdity as the rationalist in fact supposes it to be. In the light of sophiology it will cease to appear such, so we may say that the very dogma of Christology rests on sophiological foundations.

Obviously, in humans, created Wisdom is obscured by sin; but Christ, the second Adam, assumed a human nature exempt from sin, and so adequate to its divine prototype. But the very possibility of God's taking human nature and uniting it with his own, rests upon the essential conformity between the two; and that, in its turn, rests upon the unity in diversity of Wisdom, in God and in the created world. That diversity can never abrogate this unity or analogy: this is primary.

How then are we to conceive the one life of the God-human in its two natures, "inseparable and unconfused"? Theology furnishes an applicable general notion in the doctrine of "kenosis" based upon the texts Phil. 2.5, 6.2, Cor. 8.9, and Eph. 2.10–17; 5.7–8. So St. Cyril of Alexandria says: "The Word willingly gave himself to be spent and of his own will stooped to our likeness, not ceasing to be what he is, but withal *while continuing God he did not disdain the measure of manhood...for wherein did he humble himself, if he abhorred the measure of manhood?*"[3]

How are we to conceive this kenosis of the Word? In the first place it is essential to realize that, contrary to the various kenotic theories of Protestantism, our Lord in his abasement never ceased to be God, the Second Person of the Holy Trinity. At the same time, we understand his humanity to have been capable of so embodying his divine life that he was in truth both Son of God and Son of Man. And between these two terms there must be some connection, an identity in distinction. This is found in Divine-humanity, that unity of eternal and created humanity which is Sophia, the Wisdom of God.

That the Son of God "came down from heaven" means that he confined that mode of existence which was his as heavenly Wisdom to the measure of its creaturely existence in humans, to the end that he might then raise the creaturely up to the heavenly in the state of his glorification. He abandons "the glory he had...before the world was" (John 17.5). That Glory he gains from the Father again when "the Son of man is glorified" (John 13.31). Then only he says, "All power is given unto me in heaven and in earth" (Matt. 28.18). But this glory of his is itself, since it is his divinity, divine Wisdom, and that in the Trinity means the Spirit revealing the Word. In the

---

3. Explanation of the fourth anathematism against Nestorius.

Incarnation the Word divests himself of this glory, and confines the life which is his in divine Wisdom within the measure of the created wisdom in process of coming to be. *He remains in the nature of God, but devoid of his glory.* This sharing our nature and life, in which the kenosis of the Son consists, is a divine sacrifice, an incomprehensible wonder of the love of God for creation, "which things the angels desire to look into" (1 Peter 1.12).

Together with this metaphysical kenosis we must take into account the further earthly, human kenosis involved in following the path of obedience even unto the death of the cross. The God-human lived his own life throughout along the line of this simultaneous self-abasement on two levels. Christ our Lord underwent all the limitations and infirmities of human life. He was subject to every human propensity which does not involve sin: he experienced hunger and thirst, exhaustion, grief, temptation— though without yielding to this last. He himself bore witness to his ignorance, or at least the limitation of his knowledge to the measure of human inference. He continually prayed to his Father in heaven as God. His mighty works, his miracles, he performed in the power of the Spirit and of prayer, showing himself in this "a prophet mighty in deed and word."[4] He performed his ministry as teacher and prophet, imparting divine Wisdom in human terms. And finally he fell into the hands of his human enemies and was betrayed to death.

He himself claimed to be the Son of God. Yet even this apprehension of his own personality remained subject to the conditions of human growth. Of his childhood it is

---

4. See Bulgakov, *On Miracles in the Gospel, A Christological Sketch.*

said that "the child grew and waxed strong in spirit, filled with wisdom: and the grace of God was upon him: (Luke 2.40). "He increased in wisdom and stature, and in favor with God and man" (52). Times and seasons had their effect upon his life. It was throughout a life of obedient service, of *oboedientia activa et passiva* (obedience both active and passive), till it led him to the agony of Gethsemane and to Golgotha.

The agony provides clear evidence at once of the reality of his human nature and of the depth of his self-abasement: Christ our Lord there subjects his human nature, "sorrowful even unto death," to the will of the Father, expressed within him as the voice of his own divine will. There, in his human nature the representative human feels the force of the sin of the whole world pressing upon him, the horror, for the one sinless being, of contact with sin, and of the justice of God outraged thereby. He took upon himself the sin of the world in this way because he had already made himself one with all humankind. As the second Adam, his human nature is universal. Metaphysically, this was a consequence of the Incarnation. Spiritually, it was the work of compassionate love. Thus to endure the horror of sin and of the wrath of God directed against it was already spiritually to have accomplished the redemption of humankind. But such a spiritual redemption alone was not enough; there is the animal-bodily being of humankind to be taken into account as well. It was this which required his dreadful bodily sufferings and abandonment to death, with the final dereliction. The cry which resounded from the cross at the moment of his death, "It is finished" (John 19.30), marked the last depth of his abasement, and signified that it too was finished.[5] From that point his glorification takes its start.

For a right understanding of the kenosis, it is essential to grasp the fact that the glorification of Christ is at once his own achievement in virtue of his obedience to the end, and an effect produced in him by the action of the Father, making him worthy and capable of receiving it. In the former sense it is natural to take the series of texts which refer to the Resurrection: Matt. 28.6; Luke 24.34; Rom. 8.34; 1 Cor. 15.34; in the latter sense the corresponding series: Acts 2.24, 32; 3.15, 26; 4.10; 5.30; 10.40; 8.30, 32, 34, 37; 17.31; Rom. 4.24; 10.9; Col. 2.12; 2 Cor. 4.14; Gal. 1.17; Eph. 1.20; 2.5-6; 1 Thess. 1.10 (with which cf. 1 Peter 1.21). The same distinction holds good for the Ascension, on which we have, on the one hand, Matt. 16.19; Luke 24.50; and, on the other, Acts 2.23; Eph. 1.19, 20. In such passages Christ is spoken of at once as rising and raised by the Father, ascending and received up by the Father. This indicates that the Son's abandonment, in his kenosis, of his divine power and glory, is prolonged even beyond the term of his earthly ministry. The grant of immortality to his glorified body, and through him to the rest of humankind at the resurrection, is likewise a new creative act of God. But it is not a new creation *ex nihilo*. It is merely the communication of the gift of immortality to human nature, itself already created and remaining, at present, subject to death, but now rendered worthy and capable of receiving such a gift by the obedience which Christ

---

5. Actually the last act of this process was the preaching to the "spirits in prison." We do not propose to dwell upon that here.

freely offered his Father. "Jesus of Nazareth...God hath raised up, having loosed the pains of death: because it was not possible that he should be holden of it" (Acts 2.22, 24).

And the final, conclusive stage of the kenosis extends even into the heavens, during those ten days between the Ascension and Pentecost, while the Son "prays" the Father to send the Holy Spirit. It is then brought to an end only when the Son is sent the Spirit from the Father. Christ, having left the world, henceforward sits as the God-human at the right hand of the Father in Glory, until the time comes for his second and glorious coming, the Parousia.

What does this prolongation of the abasement and the exaltation alike of the God-human signify in regard to the hypostatic union of the two natures? From our point of view, what is its bearing on the relation between the divine and the created Wisdom? The distinction between the two natures persisted throughout the period of his earthly ministry. It was then necessary for his human nature to be brought into accord with the divine, with divine Wisdom. For he took that nature in its created form and, as such, was impaired by the effects of sin, irrespective of his personal sanctity and sinlessness and his virginal conception exempt from original sin. The actual condition of human nature by no means reflected, as yet, its origin in Wisdom. Wisdom, present in it in principle, had yet to be realized. To put it in the ordinary language of Christology, we may say that Christ's human nature retained its own will, beside and below his divine will. But for this human will to "follow" the divine required a sustained endeavor, the supreme effort of which was exerted in the prayer of the victim contemplating his sacrifice in Gethsemane, as witnessed by the cry, "not my will, but thine be done" (Luke 22.42). "Thy" will is here the one divine will, common to Father and Son alike; "my" will, distinguished from the Father's by its very obedience, is the human will of the God-human, bowing down to it. Christ our Lord in his ministry fully and entirely actualized all the potentiality of divine Wisdom even in his human nature; and it is with that in view that he is called "Christ, the power of God and the wisdom of God."[6]

In the substantial unity of the God-human created Wisdom is fully united and identified with the divine, yet without overthrowing the fundamental ontological distinction between the two natures, the divine and the created. And to eternity they remain thus distinct, as the expression of the Incarnation and the resultant "composite" nature of the God-human. But in his state of glory they attain to that complete concord and interpenetration which is described in Eastern patristic literature as *perichoresis*, the *communicatio idiomatum*. This expresses the fullness and unity of that life, at once divine and human, which Christ now lives, and which is to be extended, in the final fulfillment, to the whole world, the whole of Divine-humanity. He himself, Christ our Lord, has raised humanity not merely to the degree of glory which it enjoyed before the Fall (Rom. 3.23), but to a state of full divinization, theosis, whereby "God shall be

---

6. This phrase (1 Cor. 1.24) cannot be adduced as proof that Wisdom is to be identified in particular with the Second Person of the Trinity, the Word, except through failing to notice that it refers not to the Word but to Christ, that is, to the God-human in the sophianic unity of his two natures.

all in all" (1 Cor. 15.28). But this divinization, though evidently a result of the Incarnation and the work of the grace of God, yet cannot be without some ontological ground as well. Nothing can be divinized which has not the capacity and ontological aptitude to receive such a gift, which does not bear within itself some intimate exigency of such an end—in Aristotelian terms, its entelechy. Divinization can result neither from some mechanical impulse from without, some *Deus ex machina*, nor from unnatural constraint.

The union of natures, with its accompanying *communicatio idiomatum*, presupposes their original conformity. And we discover this conformity in interpreting the two natures in Christ as the two forms of the one Wisdom of God, those which it takes respectively in God and in creation. Christ's created humanity is rendered transparent to his eternal humanity. From the God-human shines forth very God in his Glory, the light of the everlasting Godhead, divine Wisdom. In him, indeed, for the first time the true idea of Divine-humanity, according to the conception of the Creator, is realized in its integrity, in the unshadowed clarity of its form. For Divine-humanity is the unity and complete concord of the divine and the created Wisdom, of God and his creation, in the person of the Word.

The dynamic aspect of this union of the two natures in Christ means that in him God is redeeming humankind, reconciling the world unto himself. Christ, the high priest, having entered into the heavenly places by his blood, pleads for our sins before the Father; and this sacrifice of our redemption, offered out of time, and therefore for all time, finds its completion in the world in the mystery of the Holy Eucharist. All the humanity of Christ which has still to gain the state of Glory, all humankind which has ever lived, is living, or has yet to live, remain united in a dynamic unity with him, and so far constitute the Church, the body of Christ. And in this way the withdrawal of Christ from the world at the Ascension does not mean that he is separated from it (John 14.18, 19); it is quite compatible with his continued connection with and abiding presence in the world, as, indeed, he himself testifies: "All power is given unto me in heaven *and* in earth" (Matt. 28.17). This "and" points to the link between heaven and earth, to Divine-humanity, the unity of divine and created Wisdom. This unity is realized in the progressive penetration of the world by Wisdom, bringing it gradually into conformity with its prototype in Wisdom.

This process is accomplished in the continuance in the world of that ministry of Christ which he has already fulfilled in person in his life in the world. It is a ministry at once prophetic, in the Word, priestly, in the Sacraments, and regal, insofar as Christ is crowned king of kings over all the world. And its effect is to bring the world into conformity with the divine plan for it, and so to manifest it as the creaturely Sophia, the Wisdom of God. Christ's connection with the world, since the Ascension, is realized sacramentally, over and above his presence throughout the Church by the Holy Spirit (see below), through his real presence in the Holy Eucharist, until the moment of his visible manifestation at his second coming, in the Parousia.

The change of the holy gifts in the Eucharist denotes the inclusion of the "elements" of this world in the glorified body of Christ, for that body, though now taken from the world and abiding "in the heavens" is no longer limited by time and space and is capable of appearing on every altar everywhere and at all times. This glorified body answers to the human nature in Christ, wholly divinized through its union with the divine in the one person of the Word. Or, to put it another way, it answers to the nature of created Wisdom in the God-human, which belongs to this created world, and stands for its glorification in Wisdom. The created world has still far to go before the likeness of Wisdom appears in it; nevertheless, it bears that likeness hidden within it. In the human nature of Christ, on the other hand, this likeness is already absolutely clear. Here, then, we have the identity and distinction of the two forms of created wisdom at once. As in the Incarnation the manifestation in union of the two natures finds its foundation in their conformity in Wisdom as divine and as created, so too the eucharistic change, *metabole*, has its foundation in the *unity* of created nature, whether glorified or not. In becoming human Christ forged in his own body a link with the whole world of "flesh"; it all now forms a potential extension of his body. The full significance of this link will be disclosed only at his second and glorious coming; till then it is manifested sacramentally, and, to fleshly eyes, invisibly, in the Eucharist, the primary effect of which, indeed, is to give us a personal union with Christ. But it also signifies the eucharistic presence of Christ in the world.[7]

---

7. See Bulgakov, *The Eucharistic Dogma.*

5

Pentecost
and Divine-humanity [1]

God's self-revelation in the Holy Trinity is effected through the generation of the Son and procession of the Holy Spirit from the Father. Accordingly this self-revelation of the triune God is common to the Word and the Spirit alike, the two persons together disclosing the Father in one revelation—Sophia. Sophia reveals not the Logos, or Wisdom in person, alone, nor the Spirit, the personal Spirit of Wisdom, alone.

The content of this self-revelation belongs to the Word, its life and its being to the Spirit; the former is Truth, as the latter is Beauty. Truth cannot exist isolated from Beauty; nor Beauty outside of or parted from Truth. It is not the ideal world of thought, a lifeless abstraction alone, nor is it living reality devoid of all content and opaque to thought, which forms the content of such self-revelation. All thought without vigorous life is

---

1. For the whole of this chapter see Bulgakov, *The Comforter*, chapters IV-V.

but dead and schematic, while life devoid of its content of thought is blind, elemental. The Wisdom of God, as the self-revelation of Godhead, is live, vital thought, the word of the Word, upon whom the power of the Spirit abides.

Sophia is the heavenly type of humanity or, in this sense, heavenly humanity itself. Hence this latter is also a common revelation of the Logos and Spirit, disclosing both persons together. According to Gen. 1.27, humans are made in the image and likeness of God in a twofold embodiment, the masculine and feminine principles. These in themselves are not to be identified simply with sex and the sexual life, for this exhibits a sinful deterioration of the relations between these two principles, a clothing of human nature in "coats of skins." This duality of the masculine and the feminine principles in humans, which corresponds to the primacy of reason or thought in masculine, and of heart and feeling in feminine nature, does not divide human nature, though it inwardly diversifies it and thus goes to make up its fullness. The masculine and feminine principles in humanity subsist unconfusedly, while admitting of identification in some form of spiritual union. Yet they are at the same time inseparable, not only in the sense that either apart from the other does not possess human nature complete, but also in that the spirit of every human being combines elements of this dual principle, though of course in different ways and in different proportions. This feature of humankind as created in likeness to God undoubtedly finds its analogy in heavenly humanity, Sophia. Though here, of course, we can hardly apply in all rigor the earthly distinctions between the two principles present in

99

humans, yet no more can we rob of its force the analogy between type and prototype. In particular, we must take into account two complementary facts. On the one hand, the Logos assumed human nature precisely in its masculine, not in its feminine, or even androgynous, form. On the other hand, we have the Church, with the Virgin of course at its head, symbolized chiefly by feminine figures, as in the Song of Songs, in the Apocalypse, and in Ephesians.[2]

The world is created, as we saw above, by God the Father, who in the beginning, that is, in Sophia, the Son and Spirit concurring, spoke the creative word: "let there be" this or that. The Holy Spirit is dwelling unseen in the world, as its quickening force and reality. But he is present there not only thus to establish the world in its distinct existence and life, but also to elevate humanity, once inspired by himself, all the way to the heights of divine inspiration: "Who spake by the prophets." Under the old dispensation even before the descent of the Word the Spirit was sent to the world from God, from the Father, though, clearly, not in his person; he was sent through his gifts, working as Wisdom on humans, in whom wisdom is immanent by their creation. The Old Testament knows various forms of the gifts of the Spirit, of God: the spirit of battle, of kingship, of art, no less than of prophecy. This was already Divine-humanity in process of being accomplished under the old dispensation before the Incarnation. This outpouring of gifts of

---

2. Here it is natural to note that in the Syrian writers of the fourth century, Afraat, for example, and in the old Syriac versions, we find the Third Hypostasis spoken of frankly as feminine, the Syriac term for "spirit," unlike the Greek and the Latin, being feminine.

the Spirit effected a union of natures between God and humans, as it were, by anticipation, in the spiritual life of an elite of humankind. This union, however, was still not complete; it did not extend to the animal-bodily life.

The Word was not fully made flesh till he came down from heaven and was conceived by the Virgin; and this, too, was the act of the Spirit as well. In the Annunciation both the Word and the Spirit are sent from the Father to reveal Sophia to the world, and thus to reveal, in the earthly, the heavenly humanity. The next point to note in this mystery is that the Spirit must come on the Virgin, and be accepted by her, before she can conceive and give flesh to the Word. Her divine infant is only conceived in the power of the Spirit: it is not that the Spirit is given to crown his conception. In the Incarnation the Son and the Spirit come down from heaven together, for the Spirit, who rests on the Son inseparably and unconfusedly, in his descent on the Virgin brings down the Word too in person, in virtue of which she, conceiving the Son, becomes the birthgiver of God.

The Holy Spirit, who thus eternally rests on the Son and is therefore inseparable from his divinity, while by "grace" (Luke 2.40) he rests also upon his humanity, at the Savior's baptism further descends on the latter in person. And thereby our Savior becomes in the full sense the Christ, and receives the anointing of the Holy Spirit, who thus remains with him during the whole of his ministry. And here let us repeat once again it is as the incarnate Word thus anointed with the Holy Spirit that Christ, in Sophia the twofold revelation of both divine persons, appears as the Power and Wisdom of God (1 Cor. 1.24). The withdrawal of Christ from the world, in consequence of his ascension and sitting upon the right hand of the Father, is from the first associated with the sending of that other Comforter whom in the last discourse he promised to send; there follows the actual descent of the Spirit at Pentecost. The full force of this fact too can only be seen in the light of the doctrine of Divine-humanity or of Sophia.

First of all we must grasp the relation between the persons of God involved in this mission. The originating Hypostasis throughout remains, as before in all missions *ad extra,* the Father. Yet in fulfilling their mission, the other two persons completely change places. When the Word became flesh, the Spirit accomplished the will of the Father to send him, and, so far, himself seemed to send him. By contrast, at Pentecost, it is the Son who, it seems, sends the Spirit when he promises to "pray the Father" concerning this Comforter, that, in the name of the Son, the Father would send him (John. 15.16, 26). The fact that the days of his flesh are accomplished completes the circle and opens a new possibility for the descent of the Holy Spirit into the world, through the mediation of the Son.

Though the Word and the Life, the Son and the Spirit, are two, yet the bond which unites them appears in the one self-revelation they share in Sophia, alike in eternal Divine-humanity in God and in the appearing in time among human beings of the God-human. The other Comforter is sent into the world not to bring it some new revelation, his own, but to bring to completion that made by the Son; the content revealed is precisely the same for them both. And this is expressed with great force in our Savior's promise to send him: the two "Comforters" are distinct persons, inseparable as unconfused; the comfort they bring is the same. The Comforter when he descends brings to the world life in Christ, proclaims Christ, is the "Spirit of Christ" (1 Peter 1.11) of whom it can be said: "Now if any man have not the spirit of Christ, he is none of his" (Rom. 8.9); "That the God of our Lord Jesus Christ, the Father of glory, may give unto you the Spirit of wisdom and revelation in the knowledge of him" (Eph.1.17); "The Spirit of Jesus" (Phil 1.19; with which compared Gal. 4.6, and I Peter 1.10–12). Christ says of the Comforter, "He shall teach you all things, and bring all things to your remembrance, whatsoever I have said unto you" (John 14.26); "He shall testify of me" (15.26). And, finally, a text which sums up all this reads as follows: "Howbeit, when he the spirit of truth is come, he will guide you into all truth: For he shall not speak of himself; but whatsoever he shall hear, that shall he speak, and he will show you things to come.... All things that the Father hath are mine: therefore said I that he shall take of mine, and shall show it unto you" (16.13, 15). In such Fathers as the great Athanasius and Basil, we find the same thought expressed thus: the Son is the image of the Father, the Spirit is that of the Son. A further fact, too, supports this. When Pentecost came, and even immediately afterward, the sole and entire theme of the apostles' preaching was neither the Holy Spirit nor the fact of Pentecost, but the suffering and glory of Christ (cf. the first sermon of Peter, Acts 2.22–36).

Inevitably the question arises—what sense can we put upon such references to the Holy Spirit, which seem to attribute to him such an entirely subservient and secondary place, compared with the incarnate Word? The Holy

103

Spirit appears to have no more to do than to spread the good news of the God-human, and minister to him. As to this we need only point out that it answers at all points to the converse relation that held at our Lord's Incarnation, which the Holy Spirit prepared and announced and led up to. Then there is no question of "subordination." In giving flesh to the Word, the role ascribed to the Spirit certainly does not belittle him. The mutual relation between the Son and Spirit in the Incarnation is evidence only of the double part played therein by Sophia, as heavenly and creaturely humanity at once. The whole revelation is one: the personal Word brought to fruit by the Holy Spirit; and therefore this same Word is preached by the apostles, when moved by the Spirit. Yet this sort of transparency, in virtue of which it is the Word, not himself, which the Spirit reveals in himself, in Divine-humanity, is thoroughly consonant with that particular aspect of love in the Godhead which distinguishes God, the Third Person. Life in the Spirit is then life in Christ, the inspiration of the Spirit gives knowledge of Christ, he who has not the Spirit of Christ is "none of his." So closely are the two persons identified in this one revelation they share.

What was it that happened at Pentecost? What sort of barrier divides the whole life of the world up to and after that moment? From the beginning the spirit of God was at work in the world, and his gifts were bestowed, in particular, under the old Covenant, and, still more, in the Incarnation of Christ. The new thing which happened at Pentecost was that there then entered the world not the "Spirit of God" in his gifts, but God the Spirit in person. Nor was the Spirit then given by measure, or bestowed on the Lord or his Mother alone, but also upon the apostles and all who were with them, and later upon the whole Church and the whole of the world. In the Holy Spirit, Christ now sent to the world from the Father that other Comforter whom he had promised to send. To grasp the full force of this happening both in itself and in its connection with the Incarnation requires some effort. The wealth of its import can be compared with nought less.

As then it was the Second Person of the Trinity which came down from heaven and took flesh, so here the Third Person comes down to abide in the world. This coming from heaven is, on the one hand, in substance the same in each case; on the other, the mode of its doing in each case is different. The difference is plain: while the Word is incarnate, the God-human revealed in person, the Spirit is neither. Instead, he permeates humanity, abides with it, makes it divine. But the realization of Divine-humanity, by such a union between the divine and the human that creaturely humanity may share in the life of the heavenly Divine-humanity, is the end of both missions alike. In other words, each is a union, and even identification, of Sophia divine and created, which yet maintains the distinction between their two natures. In the Incarnation, created Sophia, earthly humanity, receives in the Logos the personal Wisdom of God. At the descent of the Spirit the same human nature receives the personal Spirit of Wisdom. The fullness of Divine-humanity can be achieved only through both events in conjunction, just as divine Sophia itself stands for revelation effected in the persons of either disclosing hypostasis, not in that of the Son or the Spirit alone, but in both in conjunction. If Divine-humanity had to depend on the Incarnation alone for its realization, it must remain uncompleted. The same would be true if the gifts of the Spirit alone were in question, as in the Old Testament, or even the personal descent of the Spirit alone to the world. This latter in any case would be impossible had not the Incarnation preceded it. It is the Son who sends to the world from the Father the Spirit, the fruit of his own Incarnation. Here we are faced with the real connection between these two acts, the Incarnation and Pentecost, and it is plain it reflects the relation between the two persons as such, in the Trinity, and in Sophia. Inseparably and unconfusedly united, both persons reveal the Father alike in eternal Wisdom and in creation, which is called into being by the Father, through the medium and participation of both. Hence the salvation and deification of that creation in Divine-humanity can be accomplished only through both in conjunction. More than this, the personal mission of either was effected only by the aid of the other. This we have already observed in regard to the Word taking flesh, who was sent by the Father and given flesh by the Spirit. But Pentecost shows the same feature, when through the Son the Spirit is sent by the Father, so that the Spirit would seem to be sent as the direct result of the prayer of the Son to the Father. Here the Son and the Spirit, it seems, exactly reverse their previous relation.

Why is this so? It is because the historic descent of the Holy Spirit into the world at large only became possible as a consequence of the Incarnation. As a result, when the Holy Spirit comes into the world, it is as if he were coming upon Christ Incarnate once more. In the Holy

Trinity he eternally rests on the Son; on Christ the Incarnate Word he rests in his ministry and subsequent glorification at the right hand of the Father—for the Holy Spirit, whose hypostatic love unites Father and Son, himself is this *dextera Patris,* the heavenly glory bestowed on the God-human. But the Son who, at his ascension to heaven, appears to abandon the world and humankind, does not then in fact become dis-carnate, nor does he relinquish his humanity or cut himself off from the rest of creation. For the time being his personal manhood, no less than his risen body, has been removed from the world, yet in the world remains the humanity which belongs to him as the second Adam, already bound to him forever, and likewise bound up with the world. This new humankind belongs to Christ and is predestined with him to be deified. Nevertheless, it is left orphaned when first the Ascension has the Lord taken away from it.

This link with Christ, this life in him, this present reality of his Divine-humanity in the world and its destined fulfillment, provide the field for the activity of the Holy Spirit upon his descent into the world. It is for this that the Holy Spirit is sent by the Son from the Father: to bring to completion the work of Christ, to manifest him to the world, and to glorify the creature, even as the Father glorified the Son, by thus sending him. It is precisely as glory that he is sent to the world. That the Third Person of the Trinity descends into the world at Pentecost, not merely in the gifts then bestowed, but in person, is evident alike from the direct promise of our Lord in his last discourse and from many other passages of Scripture (1 Cor. 12.11; 2.10–11; Rom. 8.26–27; Eph. 4.30; Acts 13.2). It is true that the Spirit's hypostasis in this, unlike that of the Son, remains hidden from us. In the present age the Holy Spirit is revealed to us only in his gifts, in "grace." The significance of the personal descent of the Holy Spirit at Pentecost remains a mystery to us, though Pentecost is, as it were, now prolonged in the history of the Church, and in the hidden depths of the Church the process is already completed; the Holy Spirit in person has entered the world and abides in it.

But the actual manner of his descent and abiding differs from that of the Incarnation. The "descent from heaven" of the Son is accompanied by his kenosis. He voluntarily forsakes his glory, divests himself of his divine prerogatives. He seems, in fact, to leave heaven, though this by no means implies any cessation or interruption of the life of the deity in the Logos himself. This process is reversed later by his return to heaven at the Ascension. The descent of the Holy Spirit involves no such kenosis. He in his descent from heaven does not forsake it—he does not lessen his divinity and his glory. For indeed the Holy Spirit is himself the glory of the Godhead. The Holy Spirit coming down from on high, without leaving heaven, completes the link between God and creation, initiated in the Incarnation. Yet, as the Incarnation required the *personal* descent of the Son, so here the action or gifts of the Spirit alone would not be enough. His *personal* coming was needed. This inner connection between the work of the Incarnation and the bestowal of the gifts of the Spirit is vigorously emphasized in the last discourse of our Lord.

We are faced with the fundamental fact that two hypostases, and not one, are sent from on high to the world. Divine-humanity in process of being accomplished presupposes the union of the divine and human natures, or of divine and created Wisdom, in the one hypostasis of the Logos. But this union has to be effected by the Holy Spirit, more than that, *is* Holy Spirit. And this bond will be ultimately realized and sealed in the life of Christ in humanity and humanity in Christ. The consummation of this union, which is, as it were, a new manifestation or renewal of Christ's Incarnation, is the descent of the Holy Spirit. Descending from heaven, it is as though he brought the Incarnate Christ afresh in the capacity of "another Comforter" (John 14.16–18). This points to the mystery of Christ's abiding in the world in the Holy Spirit; never is Christ separated from the Holy Spirit. So Divine-humanity, like the Incarnation itself, is the work not of one person, but two—the Son and the Spirit together. This principle of duality holds good alike for the divine and the creaturely Sophia, or Divine-humanity, and for the manifestation of God in the world. Christ and the Holy Spirit together are the one Comfort, although the Comforter is two in one: one Divine-humanity, accomplished in two hypostases.

The Holy Spirit descends into the world once for all, never to return or be withdrawn from it. On the contrary, we see that he makes ready for the second coming of Christ into the world, as Divine-humanity manifest. This coming will bring with it that hypostatic revelation of the Holy Spirit, which is not given to us in this present age, insofar as the abiding presence of the Holy Spirit in the world manifests itself only as yet in his gifts. These gifts are many and various. What they are appears, though by no means exhaustively, in the Acts as well as the Epistles. All there appear as divine inspiration of human beings, a union between inspired human endeavor and divine inspiration, bestowed in response to it. It is accomplished, as it were, in the coincidence of two principles, *ex opere operantis* (from the work worked) and *ex opere operato* (from the work of the person working). But the action of the Holy Spirit is by no means restricted to the realm of the spirit; it extends to the whole world of physical nature, sanctifying and transfiguring it from within. So, too, the Parousia, the second coming of Christ, is accomplished by a transfiguration of the world, by the vision of a new heaven and a new earth, by the descent of the Heavenly Jerusalem. And all this is the work of the Holy Spirit, who manifests the power of our Lord's Incarnation, and acts as the Spirit of Christ.

The distinctive and characteristic feature of the action of the Holy Spirit in the world and in humankind may be said to be his *adaptability* to the creature's capacity to receive him. The Holy Spirit gives himself "by measure" and "measure for measure." It is only in relation to the Son of God, by contrast with all creation, that it is said, "God giveth not the Spirit by measure *unto him*" (John 3.34). This measure is such as not to burn up the creature, or destroy its corruptible nature, but to make it possible for it to bear the Spirit. For this reason the Holy Spirit restricts the full force of his action. In a similar manner he attunes and adapts his will to that of the creature, in analogy with the way in which the two natures in the God-human, with their two wills and two energies, were coordinated, to make the lower accord with the higher.

But in Christ this concord was established within the realm of his person, while the Holy Spirit, without becoming incarnate in separate persons, permeates them all, and extends to each individual the call: "Behold, I stand at the door and knock" (Rev. 3.20). Grace accords with human freedom, it never violates this freedom; it educates and prepares it. This voluntary self-restriction, out of love for the creature and respect for its creaturely freedom, constitutes the *kenosis* of the Third Hypostasis, which is peculiar to it by virtue of its proper part in Divine-humanity. It is beyond human comprehension or reason *how* the almighty and all-holy God can restrict himself in his action. Humankind will never be given to understand how the Absolute could restrict himself in the creation of the world. But this kenosis of the Spirit, as an aspect of sacrificial love, of necessity springs from the special form of divine ministration in which "all is given by the Holy Spirit,"[3] yet only when human freedom is willing to acquiesce and accept.

The kenosis of the Third Person thus differs from that of the Second, which in the Incarnation forsakes, as it were, its divinity, and adjusts even its proper activity to the highest measure of human nature, seen in its purity and holiness in the God-human. However, the Holy Spirit does *not* abandon his divinity and is not united with human nature, but penetrates it. But when he penetrates it he always measures his action in accordance with the weakness of the creature. The kenosis of the Son extends only to the period of his earthly ministry, and ends with his glorification. The kenosis of the Holy Spirit, strictly speaking, began with the very creation, when the Holy Spirit charged himself to preserve and to quicken the creature according to its own capacity. But

---

3. From the verses for the feast of Pentecost; cf. the *Veni Creator.*

the fullness of his kenosis only takes place at his coming at Pentecost and lasts till the fullness of Divine-humanity shall be attained, when God shall be all in all. Consequently, this epoch of kenosis extends at any rate over the whole of this present age of the "Church militant," of the kingdom of grace, which is ultimately to be succeeded by the kingdom of glory. Christ's enthronement on earth, and his kingly ministry, is accomplished and extended in the world by the power of the Holy Spirit, in whom "the Kingdom of God is come in power." This then is Pentecost: the fruit of the Incarnation, the penetration of the creature by Wisdom, the union of the divine and created Sophia in the power of the Spirit— Divine-humanity.

All that has been said above undoubtedly leads to an *eschatological* concept of Pentecost. Its full significance will only be clear in the Parousia of Christ and the transfiguration of the world. There will be no special Parousia of the Holy Spirit, for he comes into the world to remain in it; but there will be, as it were, a new manifestation of Pentecost in all its power and, most important of all, in the *personal* revelation of the Third Hypostasis, that which at present we lack. We perceive the life of the Spirit by the grace of the Spirit, and we know holiness by his holiness, but we do not know the Holy Spirit himself, we do not know his personal likeness.[4] That will become known to humankind only in the Parousia of the Son, which in this sense will be also a parousia of the Holy Spirit, the full revelation of divine Sophia in its dual aspect, and of the two hypostases which disclose the

---

4. See Ch. VI below.

Father. It follows necessarily from this that the Third Hypostasis will take a special part in the resurrection, in the last judgment and in the glorification of creation. For the "kingdom prepared from the foundation of the world" (Matt. 25.34) is precisely the Holy Spirit. In the most ancient version of the text of the Lord's Prayer we read, "May the Holy Spirit come," instead of "Thy kingdom come." For this reason, when the significance of Pentecost is expounded in St. Peter's discourse immediately after the event, he makes use of a passage from Joel which is definitely eschatological (Acts 2.16–21: Joel 2. 28–32). The promise that "God may be all in all" (1 Cor. 15.28) refers to the full manifestation of the divine in the creaturely Sophia, to that deification of the creature which is to be accomplished by the power of Christ in the Holy Spirit.

6

The Veneration
of Our Lady

T he Church venerates the Mother of God as "more honorable than the cherubim, more glorious incomparably than the seraphim," as the "heavenly Queen," whom "all the elements, heaven and earth, air and sea obey." In numberless prayers and hymns her glory and grandeurs are extolled.

The Protestant mind, by some curious insensibility, quite fails to appreciate the position which belongs to the Virgin Mary, not only in the Incarnation, but in the whole life of the Church. Our veneration of the Mother of God seems to it to border on idolatry. In this connection it is apposite to refer to the fact of her full *deification*, in virtue of which she is manifested as the heart and glory of the world. For us, the dogma of the divine maternity of our Lady is fully illumined only in the light of the doctrine of Sophia, the divine Wisdom in creation.

Orthodoxy does not share the latest Catholic dogma, the 1854 definition of the Immaculate Conception, insofar as her exemption from original sin in virtue of this "immaculate conception" distinguishes the Mother of God from the rest of humankind and seems consequently to render her incapable of imparting to her divine son the authentic humanness of the old Adam, with its need of redemption. The blessed Virgin, since she is truly human, shares with humanity both its original sin and also that inherent infirmity of human nature, which finds its extreme expression in an inevitable, natural death.

However, the force of original sin, which varies generally from person to person, is in her reduced to the point of a mere possibility, never to be actualized. In other words, the blessed Virgin knows no *personal* sin; she was manifestly sanctified by the Holy Ghost from the very moment of her conception. In numerous liturgical texts, such as those which refer to her conception, nativity or presentation, she is called "the spiritual heaven," "holiest of the holy," "divine and most pure temple of the spirit," "pure from her infancy," and so forth. More than that, she is spoken of as "mother elect before all ages, made known as mother of God unto succeeding years," "beloved by God from all eternity." With this accords also her final glorification when her son honored her death by her resurrection and assumption into heaven, a doctrine contained in the office for the feast of the Dormition.

This glory is bestowed upon the blessed Virgin only in view of her part in the Incarnation. Consequently, we can distinguish a twofold act. There is the descent of the Word from heaven to become a human being and assume his human nature, which is announced by the lips of the blessed Mother of God: "Behold the handmaid of the Lord; be it unto me according to thy word" (Luke

1.38). But for that to be possible, there must already have appeared upon earth a human being worthy of the archangel's mission in the Annunciation and capable of responding to it. The whole force of righteousness, accumulated in the Old Testament church by a line of saints (the "genealogy"), was here united with her personal exceeding holiness and humility of heart.

Mary was manifestly apt for the Holy Ghost to descend upon her. But he eternally abides upon the Son. Therefore, in receiving the Spirit she, at the same time, conceived the Son, who is inseparable from him, and became Mother of God. Her humanity became his humanity.[1] In Christ this human nature was united with the divine nature, received the divine personality of the Word, and was taken up into Divine-humanity. In Mary this same human nature which she gave to Christ remained in its original human condition, with the personality of the Virgin, though now sanctified by the Holy Ghost and becoming Spirit-bearing. The birth of Christ from the Virgin is not merely an isolated event in time; it establishes an eternally abiding bond between Mother and Son, so that an image of our Lady with her infant in her arms is in fact an image of Divine-humanity.

The fact that our Lady is Spirit-bearing did not make her theandric nor constitute an incarnation of the Holy Ghost. For the Holy Ghost is not the subject but the principle, of the Incarnation. He abides, however, in the

---

1. In the prayer of St. Simeon the Meditative, in preparation for Holy Communion, we read: "Thou didst take upon thyself by the infusion of the Holy Ghost and at the good pleasure of the everlasting Father, together with the pure and virginal blood of her who bare thee, our whole compound nature."

ever-virgin Mary as in a holy temple, while her human personality seems to become transparent to him and to provide him with a human countenance. We must distinguish the different stages in this overshadowing of the Virgin by the Holy Ghost.

First of all, in this connection, comes her peculiar and exclusive sanctification by the grace of the Holy Ghost, shown in her conception, nativity, and presentation in the temple, and throughout her holy childhood and maidenhood. Next follows the personal descent of the Holy Ghost at the Annunciation, which consecrated her whole bodily being and made of her the Mother of God.

The consecration of the temple of her body could not, of course, be accomplished without a further sanctification also of her soul. The end was not yet, however; she had soon, in company with her son, and treading in his footsteps, to travel the road of his earthly ministry, to receive the "sword in her heart" all the way to her station by the cross on Golgotha, where she had to suffer a spiritual death with him upon the cross, in order, with him, to enter into his glory. She completed this entry into the glory of her son at Pentecost. Then, together with the apostles, but of course in superabundant fullness, she received the outpouring of the Holy Spirit. And this in turn prepared her for the prolongation and consummation of her glory at her falling asleep. For her it was a second Pentecost—she had had her first at the Annunciation. Now she became wholly possessed by the Spirit, and received from Christ that glory which he had from the Father, for those to "behold," as he said, "whom thou has given me" (John 17.34), and first of all his Mother. It is in the setting of this process of glorification that we must understand also the resurrection and assumption into heaven of the Mother of God. Both alike are essentially *anticipations* of what is prepared for the humanity of the whole Christ in the risen life; both were bestowed in advance upon the Mother of God at her assumption. Although following the law of human nature, she tasted natural death, yet "death could not detain her," for her humanity is at the same time that of Christ himself, who is the well of life.

As he is risen, so she, too, has her resurrection, though of course, otherwise than he who is the God-human. She was raised by him in the same way as, at his second coming, he is to raise all humankind. This resurrection of his mother Christ, of course, accomplishes, like the future general resurrection, in the power of the Holy Spirit, "the giver of life." For her, it manifests her peculiar dignity of spirit-bearer.[2] But the very fact that her resurrection takes place *before* that of the rest of humankind already sets her above this world and is in this sense her assumption into heaven, sometimes more narrowly defined in liturgical texts as her session "at the right hand of her Son."

Evidently, it is necessary to avoid a dogmatic identification of the assumption and the Ascension. Indeed, they must be distinguished, and even rigorously contrasted. Christ's Ascension and return to the bosom of the Holy Trinity is connected with his descent from heaven to be made human. It betokens the end of the kenosis of God

---

2. This thought finds expression in a symbol characteristic of the Western church, though not unknown also in the East, that of the glorification of the most holy Mother of God (or her Coronation), in so far as glorification is a work of the Trinity "appropriated" to the Holy Ghost.

the Son. The assumption of the Mother of God, on the other hand, is a notable, even an extreme, instance of the glorification of a creature, deified and sharing in the life of God, by participation. It by no means denotes a penetration into the Holy Trinity, which is metaphysically beyond the reach of any creature. It means no more than incorporation into the life of the Godhead: that life in Christ and through the Spirit of Christ, wherein "God shall be all in all." It is precisely this—no more, but also no less—which is denoted by the figure of her session "at the right hand" of her Son.

Indeed, the assumption of the Mother of God does not even denote any estrangement or metaphysical removal from the world, which is in fact impossible, being at variance with the law of created nature. The Church frankly testifies that the Mother of God "at her falling asleep did not forsake the world" (Troparion, Aug. 15). In spite of her assumption she will continue to belong to the world, although established in glory *above* the world, on a level, so to speak, midway between creation and the heaven of God. Her beneficent presence in, and peculiar nearness to, the world is manifested not only by the common mind of the Church at prayer, but also in her repeated appearances in miraculous images, visions granted to the saints, and so forth.

In the resurrection and assumption of our Lady the creation of the world may be said to be completed, and its end achieved: "wisdom is justified of her children" (Matt. 11.19). In her the world has already become glorious, divine, and worthy of the regard of God. The Mother of God, since she gave to her son the humanness of the second Adam, is also the mother of the race of human beings, of universal humanity, the spiritual center of the whole creation, the heart of the world. In her, creation is utterly and completely divinized, conceives, bears, and fosters God.

In relation to the Father she is named Daughter, in relation to the Word, Mother and Bride, unwedded Bride of God, while in relation to the Holy Ghost she is the Spirit-bearer, the glory of the world. In this sense she is the heart of the Church, its center and its personal embodiment. In relation to the saints, she is united with them in the Church in glory, and presents her petitions for the world, for which we unceasingly solicit her. Yet in her intercourse with heaven, sitting at the right hand of her Son, she stands higher than all the saints, and takes precedence even of the world of angels, in view of her part in the mystery of the Incarnation.

It is in this sense alone that the Church makes use of the prayer, "Holy Mother of God, save us."[3] She has been given power, as Queen of Heaven, by virtue of that power over heaven and earth which was granted to her son. Evidently the two are not identical, for the power of Christ is that which belongs to the divine person of the God-human; while to his Mother power is given corresponding to her complete deification and participation in the glory of her son.

Moreover she is the appointed intercessor for the human race, blessing them with her protecting veil in a peculiar sense, otherwise than do the saints in general by

---

3. This usage by no means connotes that our Lady is either an associate or a subaltern savior of the world. It must be understood only in conjunction with other references to her, asking the aid of her prayers. It connotes merely the singular power of her prayerful intercession—no more.

their prayers and intercessions. For the saints have still to grow in holiness, going from strength to strength along the way of progressive sanctification. And besides, they still remain on the *hither side* of the resurrection region, to reach which they await the Second Coming of Christ, while our Lady's resurrection is already accomplished. That is yet to come for them, which for her has already come to pass. She has arrived at that *fullness* of the god-like life of grace which for the rest of creation remains to be revealed. Therefore the Mother of God remains *inaccessible* to the world, for she is above the world, and if she appears to it, that is only in virtue of her loving condescension, a kind of self-abasement proper to her.

Jacob's ladder, set up between heaven and earth, was a figure of our Lady. The complete manifestation of the Mother of God to the world will only be possible when the world itself enters into the kingdom of glory in virtue of the general resurrection and all creation is transfigured. So iconography depicts the holy Mother in the last judgment at the right hand of her son, where she appears to intercede with him for a world of sinners; and, indeed, according to the belief of the Church, she does assist souls along the path which she herself travelled at her falling asleep.

The veneration of our Lady in Orthodoxy is such that those outside may well ask the question, Is not this frankly exaggerated? Does it not introduce into Christian doctrine the figure of a goddess? Such a misapprehension may be dissipated by the simple consideration that our Lady, however exalted may be the honor paid her, is not divine, is not even theandric. Her human nature and personality subsist in spite of her complete deification. Though she, upon whom the Holy Ghost reposes, is therefore spirit-bearing, yet for all that she remains a woman, however fully deified. The Holy Ghost is not personally incarnate like the Son. In conformity with his personal nature he blesses, sanctifies, penetrates, and vivifies, and that is all. And yet his fullest and loftiest manifestation is nevertheless effected in the spirit-bearing "blessed" Virgin Mary. She is, in personal form, the human likeness of the Holy Ghost. Through her, with her human form become entirely transparent to the Holy Ghost, we have a manifestation and, as it were, a personal revelation of him.

The person of the Holy Ghost remains hidden from us even in his descent at Pentecost, which conferred immediately only the *gifts* of the Spirit.[4] But there is a human person to whom it is given to manifest the Holy Ghost himself, and that is the most holy Virgin, Mary, the heart of the Church. And yet this *manifestation* of the Holy Ghost—let us emphasize the fact that it is precisely a manifestation, not an incarnation—remains for us in this life beyond our understanding.

It vanished from the world with the event of the death, resurrection, and assumption of our Lady; her glorified likeness is unknown to the world, which cannot yet receive its revelation of the Holy Ghost. It concerns only the age to come, and will belong to the last things. Together with the appearance of the glorified Christ at his coming again in Glory, the world will behold his glorified humanity in the person of the Spirit-bearer, the Virgin Mary.

---

4. For Pentecost, see my work *The Comforter.*

Divine-humanity is to be found "on earth as it is in heaven"—in a double, not only a single, form: not only that of the God-human, Christ, but that of his Mother too. Jesus-Mary—there is the fullness of Divine-humanity. The internal self-disclosure of the Holy Trinity is marked by this same duality: the revelation of the Father is made through the Son and Spirit together, inseparably and unconfusedly. In like manner, in the Incarnation, the Son is "conceived by the Holy Ghost, born of the Virgin Mary." She is the personal subject of the humanity of Christ, and his feminine counterpart. The image of the Mother of God with her child is an expression of this Incarnation of Divine-humanity. To separate Christ from his mother (still more to forget her, as historical Protestantism has done) is in effect an attempted violation of the mystery of the Incarnation, in its innermost shrine.

Yet the veneration of the Virgin extends not merely to her divine maternity, but also to herself. Accordingly she is depicted in certain of her icons apart from the Holy Child, as the "Unwedded Bride," as "Ever-Virgin."[5] This conception of her perpetual virginity is, as it were, a personification of the Church, the glorified creation, the Bride of the Lamb; and it is in this sense that the expressions of the Song of Songs concerning the mystical marriage of Christ and the Church are most often understood, alike in East and West. Rightly, then, does this figure of "created Wisdom" hold its central position

---

5. For example, the mosaic in the sanctuary apse of the ancient cathedral of St. Sophia at Kiev, known as "the Impregnable Wall," or the icon of "the Compassion," before which St. Seraphim of Sarov used to pray, excellently reproduced in A. F. Dobbie-Bateman, *St. Seraphim of Sarov*, London, 1936, and elsewhere.

in the shrine of Sophia, the Wisdom of God, at Kiev. And with this we reach the sophiological aspect of the doctrine and cultus of our Lady.

Without entering into a detailed discussion of the origin and significance of the change, it does seem to be an admitted fact of history, of considerable dogmatic interest, that the shrines of Sophia, the Wisdom of God, which for Byzantium bore a christological meaning, received a mariological interpretation in Russia. They were dedicated under the title of our Lady, and their feasts of title, in accordance with Russian usage, came to be celebrated on her feasts[6]— at Kiev on the day of her Nativity, at Novgorod and elsewhere on that of her Dormition. Thus the cult of the Wisdom of God received a marial character.

The Christ-Sophia of Byzantium was completed in Russia by a Marial-Sophia. This development found expression alike in iconography and in liturgy. Either the icons of Sophia are given a frankly marial theme[7] or they display a complex dogmatic composition in which our Lady is still assigned her place.[8] A rich field of material for this purpose is supplied by the offices of her feasts, such as her Nativity and Presentation in the temple, wherein is

---

6. It is natural to reckon as a Mario-Sophianic feast that of the Intercession of the Virgin, celebrated particularly in Russia: it refers to the protection which she extends to the world.

7. Here we must note the church icon in the cathedral of St. Sophia at Kiev—evidently of Western origin—of the Mother of God as Wisdom (following Wisd. 9.1 and ff.) and as the Church.

8. In this connection the chief significance belongs to the Novgorod compositions for an icon of Wisdom, as a fiery angel, with our Lady on the right side and St. John the Baptist on the left. See V. d. Mensbrugghe, *From Dyad to Triad*, London 1935.

disclosed her predestination from eternity,[9] her "pre-election" in the ways of Providence, which in a true sense may be set on a parallel with that of the Lamb "foreordained before the foundation of the world" (1 Peter 1.20). There even exists a proper office of Sophia, the Wisdom of God, which is combined with the office of the Dormition. Its fundamental peculiarity is that the several texts of its prayers and hymns lend a twofold significance to Sophia. The Christo-Sophianic and the Mario-Sophianic interpretation are there simultaneously present. Sophia is equated at once with Christ and with the Mother of God. This duality points to the peculiar sophiological conception which we have now to unfold with regard to the Mother of God.

It is possible to find a double source of this identification of our Lady with Sophia, the Wisdom of God, and to give it, accordingly, a twofold interpretation. In the first place our Lady can be given the name of Sophia, insofar as she is the Spirit-bearer, in virtue of the personal descent upon her of the Holy Ghost; she is his consecrated temple. Although she does not thereby become theandric, since the Holy Ghost is not incarnate, yet she is his anointed vessel. Wisdom in the Godhead is both the Son and the Holy Ghost. If the Logos is Wisdom, so too is the Holy Ghost, since he is the Spirit of Wisdom. And the cultus of our Lady as Wisdom may refer to her *position* of Spirit-bearer, not to her personally, since she is

---

9. It is characteristic that for these feasts Prov. 9 is always included among the Old Testament lessons, while on the Annunciation there is added to this Prov. 8.22–35, which adds the Mario-Sophianic interpretation of Wisdom (in reference to Christ, on the contrary, this lesson is never employed).

overshadowed by the Holy Ghost, but through her to the Holy Ghost himself. And in that sense it is to be taken as veneration of the *divine* Wisdom.

But besides this we find another meaning attached to the veneration of our Lady, insofar as it is directed to *created* Wisdom. She *is* created Wisdom, for she is creation glorified. In her is realized the purpose of creation, the complete penetration of the creature by Wisdom, the full accord of the created type with its prototype, its entire accomplishment. In her creation is completely irradiated by its prototype. In her God is already all in all. The limits to the penetration of creation by Wisdom, involved in its freedom to develop, are entirely transcended in the "handmaid of the Lord," who is already worthy of the glory of heaven. Divine Wisdom shines forth in creaturely form in the complete holiness of her who is "more honorable than the cherubim, more glorious incomparably than the seraphim." For ontological holiness is at the same time fully realized Wisdom, wherein "wisdom is justified of her children" (Matt. 11.19). In this aspect of Wisdom manifest in our Lady it is precisely her *creatureliness* which appears to be essential, her created human nature, which was found worthy to be honored with the bestowal of the Holy Ghost.

It is impossible, however, to exclude the christological aspect of this line of thought. The Mother of God is glorified with the title of Wisdom only insofar as she is Mother of the God-human, who took from her his human nature, the counterpart of created Wisdom. According to the sophiological interpretation of the definition of Chalcedon, the two natures in Christ correspond to the two forms of Sophia, the divine and the created. The created humanity of Christ the God-human came to him from the Mother of God. It belongs to her. In a true sense it is possible to say that she herself personally is this created humanity of Christ, that she is the created Sophia. The humanity of Christ belongs at once to him, since it is one of his two natures, and to her, in whom it personally subsists. And it is in this sense, as sharing the human nature of the God-human, that his holy Mother is the created Sophia. In this way the different aspects of Sophia, the Wisdom of God, its two faces, are at one in the person of the Mother of God. And this fact is reflected in the complexity of the dogmatic expression of her relationship to the Wisdom of God.

Thus it is that the most holy Mother of God is the created Sophia, and is acknowledged and venerated as such by the piety of the Church of Russia. Therefore is she exalted as "more honorable than the cherubim, more glorious incomparably than the seraphim" and, *a fortiori*, holiest of the human race. Yet even the holy Mother of God is not the only manifestation of created Wisdom.[10] Ontologically it includes, in it is grounded the existence of the whole creation, "heaven and earth," the world of angels and the world of humans. Consequently their mutual relation is that which holds between exemplar and substantial forms, as in the Platonic world of ideas and its realization in empirical fact, in becoming. Yet it is not enough to establish merely this ontological

---

10. To the doctrine of created Wisdom is consecrated my dogmatic trilogy: I. *The Burning Bush* (on our Lady); 2. *The Friend of the Bridegroom* (on St. John the Baptist); 3. *Jacob's Ladder* (on the Angels) Paris 1927, 1928, 1929, YMCA Press.

connection between creation and its source in Wisdom, for such a connection holds also for the fallen creation, even for the devil and all whom he has seduced, both angels and humans.

Created Wisdom serves not only as the foundation of creation, but also as the means of its glorification, its potential glory. The penetration by Wisdom of the creation, which itself rests upon the basis of Wisdom, is Wisdom's proper work, in the form which particularly belongs to it, that of the *sanctity* of the creature. And in this again Wisdom is at one with the holy Mother of God, who is the summit of creation, the Queen of Heaven and Earth. From this point of view the sanctity of the creature and its penetration by Wisdom are one and the same thing. Yet it is still necessary to draw a distinction.

To begin with, let us confine ourselves to the world of angels. After that probation which witnessed the fall of Lucifer and his angels, those angels who were confirmed in grace, with the archangel Michael at their head (Rev. 12.7-11) entered upon the state of glory; and since then, bearing the marks of glory, they exemplify created Wisdom in the world of bodiless spirits. Why then do even they, for all their nearness to the throne of God—so terrifying to us—yet seem to stand incomparably lower than the holy Mother of God? We must see the reason for this, on the one hand, in their present provisional relationship toward the world of humans, with which they are united in a kind of fellow humanity in virtue of the ministry which they fulfil therein (the very name "angels" signifies ministers of God to the world of humans). The Fall separated the angels from humans. The Incarnation united them anew (John 1.51) in the person of the God-human, but as yet far from completely on the part of humankind. For the rest, it still remains to undergo judgment and pass that subsequent parting of the ways before the state of glory, when angels themselves are to be judged (1 Cor. 6.3), apparently upon the execution of their service. Therefore until the glorification of humankind and the full manifestation of its Divine-humanity, even the angels do not enjoy the fullness of their glory, for they have yet part of their course to run. Meanwhile, the holy Mother of God has already attained the fullness of her glory; she is in heaven, set above the angels, who indeed worship her, as sharing with her Son the humanity of the God-human.

She has not to come to judgment. But this judgment awaits both humans and angels, who reach the term of their assimilation to humankind only with the Second Coming of Christ (Matt. 25.31). And, accordingly, what is said of the God-human extends also, though indirectly, to the Mother of God: "Being made so much better than the angels, as he hath by inheritance obtained a more excellent name than they" (Heb. 1.4). It is the *plenitude* of creation manifest in the Mother of God which makes her "incomparably" more excellent than the relatively unfulfilled world of bodiless spirits, appointed to render angelic service to the world of humans. Nevertheless, in virtue of their holiness the holy angels, with the archangel of the Annunciation at their head, appear to form the immediate entourage of the holy Mother of God; thus the liturgical chants extol her: "O thou who are full of grace, thou art the joy of every creature: the host of angels and the race of men"; thus, too, icons depict her. The angels *serve* the holy Mother of God, recognizing in her the full expression of created Wisdom. For them, too, she is their "Lady" and the heavenly "Queen."

She is united by her holiness also with the *Saints*, insofar as they, in their own holiness, display the likeness of created Wisdom, bear the marks of Christ, are sealed with the Holy Ghost, and form part of Divine-humanity. Indeed she has closer connections here than with the world of angels, for, being human, the Mother of God is Mother also of the whole human race, the center of humankind. But she stands contrasted to the rest of humankind and elevated above it, insofar as she abides already above or beyond the world in its present age, with death and resurrection now behind her. In her is revealed all the fullness of the glory of the world; now nothing can be added to it. And at the last agony of the age, in the terrible judgment of Christ, she will be present only in order to intercede. Even in the very greatest saints that inward discernment of good and evil must be accomplished, though almost all emerge scatheless in the power of the good. In her there is no room for any such discrimination: "Thou art all fair, my love; there is no spot in thee" (Song of Sol. 4.7).

While, of course, all the saints are sanctified by the Holy Ghost, and thereby incorporated into the life of Christ, she is the temple of the Holy Ghost himself, wherein the Son of God awaits his birth from her. And nevertheless she is encircled by those of "her own race,"[11] by the saints of humankind, whose nearness to her is measured by their sanctity. Among them, at the head of

---

11. "He is of our race" said our Lady of St. Seraphim, when she appeared to him.

all humanity sanctified by Wisdom, stand the two Johns, the Forerunner and the Divine: the latter in virtue of his position as her adopted son, gained at the foot of the cross, the former in virtue of his nearness to Christ. Only one stands nearer to him than John the Baptist, and that one is his Mother. From Christ himself the Forerunner received the designation of greatest among them that are born of woman (Matt. 11.11). The service he performed as Forerunner and Baptist, "the friend of the Bridegroom," meeting and acknowledging Christ in the days of his flesh, sets him above the apostles, indeed above all the elect who have, to whatever degree, drawn near to Christ. His ministry is designated as that of an "angel" (Mal. 3.1, cf. Mark 1.2; Matt. 11.10; Luke 7. 27), with a mysterious suggestion that he is somehow peculiarly and personally connected with the world of angels. His sanctification by the Holy Ghost while yet in his mother's womb (Luke 1.44), the whole austere asceticism of his figure, all that spiritual strength given him in order to stand face to face with Christ, to accomplish the baptism of the God-human, to be a witness of the mysterious theophany which accompanied it and of the manifestation of Christ to the world, all combine to oblige us to recognize his exceeding personal holiness, even perhaps a personal "exemption" from sin rendering him akin to the Holy Virgin herself.

In this connection we should give heed to the witness of the Church's imagery, which commonly sets him in immediate proximity to Christ, nearer than any other saint and even the angels, with the one exception of the Mother of God. The blessed Virgin is depicted on the right hand of Christ, John the Forerunner on his left. We observe the same thing on the iconostasis dividing the altar from the nave, also too in the icon known as the Deësis (*deesis*—petition) and in the composition of various other icons. It is particularly to our purpose to note here again the Novgorod icon of Sophia, depicted in the guise of a fiery angel, with the Mother of God standing on the right, and the Forerunner on the left. These two would seem here to depict created Wisdom in conjunction with the symbolic figure of heavenly Wisdom.

And yet with all this the distinction that divides the Mother of God from the rest of creation still holds good; even the Forerunner remains as yet on *the hither side* of the resurrection. As regards his body he still belongs to this world and has to await his part in the general resurrection, whereas our Lady was raised straightway upon her falling asleep. However, the Forerunner will be present at the last judgment, according to the evidence of the Church's imagery, in a position unlike that of the generality of those who are there to be judged. He will be present as a witness, or possibly, like the holy Mother of God, as an intercessor. For of him in particular was said, by the mouth of the Judge himself: "Wisdom is justified of her children" (Matt. 11.19). In him, as in the Mother of God, the Wisdom of God is already manifest in creation.

◆

7

The Church [1]

What is the Church? This question has come to the forefront of Christian theological thought since the time of the Reformation and still today occupies unquestionably the first place therein. It is fair to say that it forms the chief difficulty in the path of the reunion movement, in its persistent endeavors to reassemble the outwardly divided fragments of the Church. Commonly, before defining the Church, theologians set out to debate and determine its various characteristics from what one may call its "phenomenology," from the existence as a fact of the "visible" Church. Comparatively few stop to consider what we may call the "ontology" of the Church, that "invisible" foundation of its existence to which the baptismal creed refers in the phrase "I believe in..." the Church. Though it has, of course, its empirically visible embodiment, the Church itself is evidently outside the scope of our empirical mode of knowledge; it is, in fact,

---

1. See Bulgakov, *The Orthodox Church*, London, 1935. Also in *Puit* (The Way) in Russian, *An Outline of the Doctrine of the Church*.

matter of faith—"the evidence of things not seen" (Heb. 11.1). The Church is more than an institution which happened to appear at a definite period in history, it is more than a congregation of people based on a true fellowship of spirit in doctrine and discipline; it is, in fact, more than the whole of its history. More than that, the Church transcends history, and belongs primarily not to time alone, but to eternity. It is not merely that it is of divine institution; its very mode of existence is divine, and its existence in God is prior to, antecedes, or, more exactly, conditions its historical existence.

The Church is properly uncreated and yet it enters into the history of humankind. That implies that it has a theandric character; it is, in fact, Divine-humanity *in actu.* According to the expression of the "Shepherd of Hermas," God created the world for the sake of the Church. That is as much as to say that it is at once the ground and goal of the world, its final cause and entelechy. The world of humans by its creation is already designated for deification, in the Incarnation and Pentecost. And this deification, which whether virtual or actual is the supreme actualization of the world, is effected through the Church, which thus appears as a ladder joining heaven and earth and conveying divine life to the creation. It follows from this that, insofar as it is grounded in God, the Church is divine Wisdom. And equally, in its earthly, historical existence, it is created Wisdom. In short, in the Church the two aspects of Wisdom mutually permeate one another and are entirely, inseparably and unconfusedly, united. The divine shines through the created Wisdom. The definition at Chalcedon of the mode of union of the two natures in Christ was at bottom a definition of the Church. The same would seem to apply to another dogma, as yet indeed unformulated, but held as a fact by the Church—the descent of the Holy Ghost at Pentecost into the life of creation and the spirit of humanity. It is not possible to reach a final understanding or a correct expression of the doctrine of the Church save by starting from the fundamental theses of sophiology.

Consequently, in order to understand the Church as a local community persisting through time and existing in different places, under the old and the new Covenants, and even, we may add, in "the barren church of heathendom" (as it is called in one of the chants of the Orthodox Church), we must remember that the Church is an object of faith, a revealed mystery, a manifold beyond human experience, a spiritual organism, "a body fitly joined together and compacted by that which every joint supplieth, according to the effectual working in the measure of every part" (Eph. 4.16). Of the Church as the ground and basis of the world it is said that God chose "us in him [Christ] before the foundation of the world" (Eph. 1.4) in "the fellowship of the mystery, which from the beginning of the world hath been hid in God, who created all things by Jesus Christ: to the intent that now unto the principalities and powers in heavenly places might be known by the church the manifold wisdom of God, according to the eternal purpose which he purposed in Christ Jesus our Lord" (Eph. 3.9–11). In this, as in other texts, the Church is plainly delineated as divine Wisdom, with its various aspects: the heavenly Jerusalem, "coming down from God out of heaven, prepared as a bride adorned for her husband" (Rev. 21.2); that "glory" which is given at the prayer of Christ (John 17) and "shall be revealed in us" (Rom. 8.18, 21); the "building of God" prepared for us, the "house not made with hands, eternal in the heavens" (2 Cor.5.1); "the kingdom prepared...from the foundation of the world" (Matt. 25.34).

The Church in the world is Sophia in process of becoming, according to the double impulse of creation and deification; the former imposes the conditions of the latter, the latter constitutes the fulfillment of the former. God created the world only that He might deify it and himself become all in all to it.

The world has already, in principle, become godly in becoming Churchly, through the twofold revelation inseparably and unconfusedly effected by the two revelatory persons of the Godhead in the Incarnation of the Word and the descent of the Holy Ghost. Thus by reference to these two mysteries its definition in terms of Wisdom displays particularly clearly the nature of the Church. And this identification—not without distinction—we find made in the Word of God.

There the Church is styled, in the first place, "the body of Christ": "Now ye are the body of Christ, and members in particular" (1 Cor. 12.29), the Church "is his body, the fullness of him that filleth all in all" (Eph. 1. 23; cf. 4.12, and Col. 1. 24). Such definitions are to be taken not as a mere comparison, a kind of metaphor, but in the most realistic sense. The Church is the Body of Christ in virtue of his Incarnation: it is the universal human nature of the second Adam, created Wisdom, inseparably and unconfusedly united in him with his divine nature, that divine Wisdom which is "the fullness of him that filleth all in all." It is in virtue of this participation with Christ in his state of Incarnation that the apostle Paul could say, in the name of every believing soul: "I live; yet, not I, but Christ liveth in me" (Gal. 2.20). Another mystical expression of the essence of the Church given in the Word of God is that it is the Bride or Spouse of Christ (2 Cor. 11.2; Rev. 19.7–8; 21. 9; 22. 7). Actually this expression has its origin in the Old Testament, in the Song of Songs, that most mysterious and most "New Testament" book in the whole Bible, and in the prophets (Isa. 54.6; 62.4; Ezek. 16). The mystical marriage there described is shown to be a mystery "concerning Christ and the Church" (Eph. 5. 32).

The relation between bride and bridegroom, and more especially between husband and wife, is defined as a bond of love joining two in one life, "one flesh" (Gen. 2.24; Matt. 19.5–6; 10.8). Accordingly it is applied to the Incarnation; directly to the mutual relation between Christ and his Mother, the "unwedded Bride"; more remotely in general to the soul of every human being. In terms of Wisdom this figure implies that the Word, who is himself the Wisdom of God, exercises a loving domination over the created Wisdom, uniting it to himself and thereby deifying it. But the latter is not thereby deprived of its own life, either natural or personal, in its multiple created personifications. And this love is mutual, though unequal, since Christ is the head; for as the husband is the head of the wife, so is Christ the head of the Church espoused to him (Eph. 5).

But besides this, the Church is further defined in relation to the Holy Ghost; to live in the Church is to be enlightened by his grace. The Church is therefore not only the body of Christ, but also the temple of the Holy

Ghost: "Know ye not that ye are the temple of God, and that the Spirit of God dwelleth in you?" (1 Cor. 3.16–17; 6.19; 2 Cor. 6.16; Eph. 21.22. Compare also the whole account of the working of the Holy Ghost through the apostles in the book of the Acts. And here we should recall that it is by the Holy Ghost that all the sacraments and sacramentals of the Church are accomplished, and especially the eucharistic change, *metabole*, as indicated in the epiklesis.) We already know the basis of this conjoint revelation of the Son and the Spirit in the Church. It is one and the same revelation, effected by the twofold mission of the two divine persons from the Father to the world. This is what makes the Church the revelation, in terms of created Wisdom, of the divine.

This union initiated by the Incarnation and the descent of the Holy Ghost is primarily sacramental. That is to say, it is accomplished primarily by means of the sacraments and above all by means of the Holy Eucharist. Though, of course, the sacraments form the regular channel of communion with God, they are by no means the only channel in such a sense as would exclude all others. We may say that in the present age the Church is the body of Christ precisely in being that eucharistic body on which are bestowed the eucharistic gifts of the Holy Ghost, the giver of life in Christ. To the Church as a whole the plenitude of the manifestations of divine Wisdom is present. Accordingly it is granted not only full communion with God in Christ in the power of the Holy Spirit, but also full communion in the divine and the created Wisdom of God. This latter is disclosed to the Church in the person of the Mother of God, together with the whole of the Church triumphant, angels and saintly humans. The full significance of the sophianic character of the Church cannot be restricted to its relation to Christ, or defined, so to speak, Christocentrically. That is why Protestantism is at fault in denying, as it commonly does, the proper place in the life of the Church to created Wisdom or, as we may say without prejudice, to the *communio Sanctorum* (communion of Saints), with the Mother of God at their head. In virtue of the common life of the Church, we find the stream of Wisdom flowing at every source into the glorified creation. But the reception of this fullness of the life of the Church is impaired wherever there is, if not a complete denial of the holiness of the Mother of God and the saints, and of the veneration due to them, yet some measure of defect in that veneration.

On the grounds we have mentioned it is thus impossible to confine the Church to the limits of the world of humans alone. We are bound to include in it that nature with which humankind is united. With the fall of humanity, "the creation was made subject to vanity" (Rom. 8. 20), and its glorification must await that of humanity. The blessings provided for such natural and artificial objects as water, fruit, and buildings, considered the first stage in their penetration by Wisdom *in the power of the Holy Spirit,* yield clear evidence of the activity of the Church beyond the limits of the world of humans. This is the preparation of nature for that transfiguration of all things, when "new heavens and a new earth" shall be revealed, wherein justice may dwell.

The Church is the heart and essence of the world, its hidden final cause. Above all it is the treasury of the gifts of grace, the source of eternal life and salvation. It is the guardian of the sacraments through that power of life which it derives by the "apostolic succession" from Christ. All this has, of course, always been taught in the doctrine of the Church. Yet there is a further cosmic, historical, and eschatological side to it to which we must give explicit expression here. The Church, since it is Divine-humanity in history and develops through history, is inseparable from the life of humankind in time. Humankind itself may forsake the Church and relapse into bondage under the elements of the world (Gal. 4.3), or into itself. Our own age, with its pagan naturalism and humanist idolatry of humanity provides a clear example of this. But the exaggerations of error cannot abrogate that truth which they pervert. And the truth remains, that humanity was really made to be lord of creation. It is called to lead the whole creation up to the glory of God; and if in its fall it became instead enslaved to creation, yet in Christ this servitude is thrown off by the power of the Spirit. The Satanic principle in humanity is only strengthened by its unspiritual technical conquest of nature "in its own name." But there is still the possibility of a good and true humanization of nature, accomplished in the name of Christ, and this forms part of those "works" which are to be done in his name by those that believe in him (John 14.12). In and through the Church, the conquest of the forces of nature, which is at present an unspiritual magic, can become Christian theurgy. Through humanity, created Wisdom can inform the formless elements, the *tohu-bohu* of matter, until it becomes an extension of the human body.

This is not to deny the original confidence of Christianity that heaven and earth are, at the end of this age, to be transfigured by the hand of the Lord. But that in its turn does not affect the necessity we are under of admitting that, *until* that transfiguration, all in history can and must be wrought out by humankind in human fashion. For in Divine-humanity is included the whole fullness of humanity, with its freedom and creativity. At the present time, the curse of secularism hangs over the whole economic and industrial process —that product of the new age (for in earlier periods of history, in heathen as well as in Christian cultures, economic activity was governed by values at bottom religious, and thus to some extent, at any rate, sanctified).

The secularist divorce of the human from the divine principle in humanity, with its sequel in the idolatry of the human, is an error; but equally false is the denial of the human principle in the name of the divine. For the divine-human character of the Church involves the complete union of both principles. A sophianic conception of the world renders impossible any such Manichean denial of the world that would treat it as evil and destined only to destruction, leaving humans nothing to aspire to but to flee the world, in the endeavor to become an unworldly, a discarnate being. In the same way, a sophianic conception of the Church necessarily extends to its power over nature, symbolized in all those benedictions which the Church itself employs. Nature is not alien to the Church; it belongs to it.

Still less can the general creativity of humans be allowed to be thus alien to the Church. A stream of influence long dominant brought to bear on human creativity an ascetic conception of Christianity, almost Manichean—and certainly far from sophianic—a conception generally suspicious of and at times frankly opposed to all such creativity, seeing in it no more than a Satanic self-aggrandizement and the surrender of humanity to the prince of this world. Evidently, however, we can also discern another fact to be set against this; the history of Christianity has marked a flowering of human creativity, for Christianity gave human beings spiritual freedom, and thereby liberated the creative element in them. The periods of dogmatic and liturgical creation were marked by a luxuriant flowering of all the human creative powers. But for some time now a fatal cleavage has been apparent in this field; the development of creativity in humanism followed the course of a really Satanic temptation to self-idolatry. And in face of this, Christianity necessarily appeared to occupy a defensive, apologetic position. So humanism remains up to the present pagan, whereas in truth it should belong to Christianity; in this sense the true humanism has yet to appear. Yet it remains true that human creativity—thought, science, art—is in its data and its principles sophianic. It is the revelation of Wisdom through humankind, and its reception in the world. Only a sophianic world-view can establish and justify the creative mission of humankind, made known to it in the fact of its humanity, with all its creative capacities. The discovery of a mode of creativity which shall be at the same time "Churchly" and free, with Christ and in Christ, inspired by the Spirit of God, is the task set to our generation. And that, too, is the legacy of the dogma of Chalcedon on the union of the divine with human nature, each in its full perfection, in Christ and consequently also in his Church. Creativity is given to humankind that it may humanize itself to the limit, before this age declines to its

end. For the ripening of history, too, is a process of fulfillment, hurrying toward that coming springtide of the last
days, when "the branch [of the fig-tree] is yet tender, and
putteth forth leaves" (Matt. 24.32).

In humanity creation is to become aware of its own
sophianic character and recognize it in intelligence, the
seminal reason of creation, and its flower. And therewith
humankind will recognize the likeness of the Wisdom of
God in himself.

Repentance for sin and the redemption bestowed by
Christ do not paralyze, but on the contrary liberate the
creative powers of humans. Thereby they, in virtue of the
image of God within them, recognize their own commu-
nal existence, not as individuals, but in the union of
humanity in the bond of its own common nature and of
a subsistent love. Such is the Church, a divine-human
community. Such is the *sobornost'* of its mystical life.
Such, too, in consequence, the *sociality* of its historical
life. We may say that all in the inner life of the Church is
soborny, all its outward life is social. The heart of all the
various forms which we find sociality assuming in com-
munal life and in culture is the manifestation of this
inward community, this *mutuality* whereby humankind is
unified to such a point that love for God and love for the
neighbor are inseparable, and the second command-
ment is "like unto" the first (Mat. 22.39).

A consequence of this fact is the social mission of the
Church, which leads it to extend its solicitude to, and to
accept responsibility for, the redemption not only of the
individual personality, but also of social life. This is not
merely the practical application of Christian ethics or an
opportune adaptation to the demand of the day: it is of

the very essence of the Church. For in reality humankind is more than a mere congeries of atomic individuals, more than their mechanical coagulation, not an
aggregate but an organism: the body of the Church, the
body of Christ. Sociality as a fact of nature is today considered to be obnoxious to Christianity or, at any rate,
irrelevant to it. But this is only a temporary misunderstanding; within and even outside the Church, there is a
growing understanding of the truth that "without me ye
can do nothing" (John. 15.5), for sociality is the
sophianic development of humankind through history.
And though the powers of evil will guard to the end the
force of their temptation toward separation, yet "the
saints shall reign with Christ" even outwardly in history
(Rev.20.1–6).

The elements of this world, the "beast" in continual
rebellion against the influence of Wisdom, appear at
their strongest in the state. This appears to be a kind of
callosity on the skin of the social body—the Great Wen.
And if it may be accepted by the Church (Rom. 13) and
even receive a conditional consecration on the supposi-
tion that the beast is really tamed and docile, yet the
beast remains by nature untameable. Continually it
aspires to become "totalitarian," and to effect the complete and unlimited triumph of its bestiality.

Therefore the state bears the likeness of "the beast that
ascendeth out of the bottomless pit," and, as such, it blas-
phemes all that is holy. Between it and the Church there
can be no peace, for the beast of the state "the Lord shall
consume with the spirit of his mouth" (2 Thess.2.5); it
will be overthrown and annihilated in "the kingdom of
the saints," though this itself be but a temporary, and, as

it were, symbolic, triumph of the Church on earth. But it is in conflict with the beast that the Church appears in its true colors as a community united on the basis of love, not by any kind of constraint, which for the state, on the other hand, is only natural. Accordingly any concordat between church and state can only be a compromise, necessarily embarrassing to the Church, which must always remain in relation to the state an anarchic force.

The history of the humanity of Christ is the history of the Church as it is figured in the Apocalypse. The apocalyptic content of history is the drama of the world conflict between the forces of Christ and those of Antichrist. And since Christ is conqueror, therefore it is the history of his victory and his conquest, the triumph of the Kingdom of God. This can also be presented in the sense of a struggle between two rival principles: the true Sophia which irradiates the world with wisdom, and the forces of evil, "Sophia fallen." The "woman clothed with the sun" and pursued by the dragon is opposed to "the great whore," "Babylon the great, the mother of harlots and abominations of the earth" (Rev. 17.5; with which compare the analogous figures of Prov. 7.6–27; and 9.13–18).

This is not the place to enter into the necessary discussion of that nicest question of theology, the problem of the nature of evil. Evil is a parasite, possessing no substantive title to existence, but subsisting by means of the *confusion* of good and evil, as shadows, and darkness itself, are only apparent by contrast with the light. Overcoming and suppressing evil therefore consists in *separating* it from good, whereupon it must inevitably languish and die. This separation is to be effected only by the ending of history, which accordingly appears in this respect to be a process of dialectic including sophianic and anti-sophianic moments. In history the accession of Christ to the Kingdom of God, which is the accomplishment of the Holy Spirit, is to take place upon the descent from heaven of the new Jerusalem. This is a figure of the union of the created with divine Wisdom. The whole world is coming to be the Church; therefore in the new city there will be no temple (Rev. 21. 22), for therein divine Wisdom, the diunity of the Son and the Spirit, is manifest in the created.

Only in the light of sophiology can we grasp the full scope of that eschatological fulfillment of all things, which is not limited to the final separation of good and evil in the last judgment at the end of this age, but, in ways invisible to us, transcends even that separation, for then God shall be all in all, and divine Wisdom fulfilled in the created. This accomplishment has an inner inevitability and predeterminacy, which yet does not suppress created freedom. For that freedom is not substantive but rather modal; it determines not the "what" but the "how," not the existence and final issue of the cosmic process, but only the manner of its accomplishment. All the positive wealth of being of any creature lies in its sophianic content. Certainly created freedom is allowed to immerse partially that content in "fallen" wisdom, but that can be only a transitory, not a definitive, condition. Wisdom, with its positive wealth of being, can compel by its attraction, "Not by might, nor by power, but by my spirit, saith the Lord of Hosts" (Zech. 4.6). Evil, like a shadow, possesses but an illusory existence, which sooner or later must disclose the vanity of its illusion. The liberty of the creature cannot stand up to the end against the compelling attraction of Wisdom, and its evident efficacity. This forms, so to speak, an "ontological argument" for the existence of Sophia, its constraining force. This power of persuasion is grounded in the long-suffering of God and wins its victories only by enduring much from the stubbornness of the creature.

The acceptance of this principle of sophianic determination by no means involves the denial of those torments "prepared for the devil and his angels" (Matt. 25) or of the freedom unto evil of those who still persist in self-assertion. But freedom unto evil has no substantive foundation, no resources to endure to eternity, and sooner or later must inevitably wither before the radiance of Wisdom.

This is by no means the idea of *apokatastasis*, the reestablishment of all things. Such a notion is for the most part a misunderstanding, insofar as the term is applied in connection with the last things to the accomplishment of all that failed to find a place earlier in the history of the world. What we are speaking of here is in any case not *apokatastasis*, but pan-entheosis, or simply pantheosis, the complete penetration of the creature by Wisdom, the manifestation of the power of Divine-humanity in the whole world. For this to take place a necessary sophianic postulate is required, which is in fact realized, beyond the limits of this age, in those "ages of ages," whose reality, though beyond our comprehension, the Church unceasingly proclaims. There will be nothing violent or mechanical about this accomplishment, nothing to violate or set aside the liberty of the creature. But the latter cannot be set side by side with or over against divine Wisdom on a basis, so to speak, of *equal* competition, for ontologically they are not equal. Yet, in effect, they are treated as equal by those who attribute the like degree and kind of perpetuity impartially to the work of Wisdom in paradise and that of the forces opposed to it in hell.

The freedom of the rebellious creature cannot stand up to the end against the divine Wisdom on the empty resources of its own nothingness. For in reality there is but one true existence, the divine. There is only the one God in his divine Wisdom, and outside him nothing whatever. What is not God is *nothing*. Yet he does not constrain freedom; he convinces it. It will be preserved inviolate even after the victory over the powers of hell. Yet that victory is to be won not by annihilation, as the theory of conditional immortality supposes, but by the liberation of those sophianic forces of life which are preserved even in the cramped and distorted existence of hell. And into the fullness of this unfolding of the riches of Wisdom must of necessity enter all that finds its proper fulfillment through history, all the self-enlargement and self-conquest accomplished by humankind. For humankind can gain wisdom only in freedom, though it be created freedom, learning with its human will and energy, as the sixth General Council defined, to "imitate" the will of God.

Freedom is only a mode in which life is participated, not the content of life itself. That can consist only in one thing: for the creature to receive and effect after its own manner, in freedom, and endlessly to prolong that realization of the divine in the created Sophia, which is the Church. "In wisdom hast thou made them all" (Ps. 104).

INDEX

Index

Index

Index

Son as inseparable from, 101
tri-unity of the divine Sophia
and, 45-53
Wisdom of God and, 45, 46
Holy Tradition, 5, 7
Holy Trinity, 18, 37. *See also* Tri-
unity of the divine Sophia
Council at Chalcedon and, 83-
84
creation of the world and, 67-
71
God-humanhood and, 80
self-revelation of God and, 60,
61
substance and, 24-25, 31-36
transcendental principle
within, 39
two basic postulates of, 23
Wisdom of God and, 57
Humanism, 7, 20
Humanity
Church and, 140-143
divine nature and, 85-90
divinization of, 94-97
image/essence of God and, 77-
81
kenosis doctrine and, 90-94
masculine and feminine principles of, 99-100
Mother of God as intercessor
for, 119-121
spirit's relationship to the body
and, 56-59
theandric nature of, 83-84

I

Immaculate Conception, 114-
115
Incarnation, 18

angels and the, 128-129
Church and the, 136-137
divine/human personality and
the, 85
divinization of humanity
through the, 82, 95-97
kenosis doctrine and the, 89-94
Mother of God sanctified by
the, 115-116
Pentecost and the, 103-110
Son and Spirit working
together in the, 101
St. Irenaeus of Lyons, 46
Isaiah (prophet) and Glory of
God, 30

J

Jacob's ladder, 121
Jacob's Ladder (Bulgakov), 127n
Jesus. *See* Christ; Logos in the
Holy Trinity; Son of God;
Word of God
St. John of Damascus, 24, 25, 64
John the Baptist, 131-132
Judgment of the world, 13,
129
Jungfrau Sophia, 6

K

Kenosis doctrine, 89-94, 108,
111-112

L

Lady of St. Seraphim, 130n
Lamb of God, The (Bulgakov),
77n, 82n
La Russie et l'église universelle
(Solovyov), 9

Index

Index

Index

Logos and, 41-45, 47-48, 51-53
self-revelation and, 51-52
self-sufficiency of God's being
   and, 73
triune hypostases and, 53
Truth, 98

U

Unfading Light, The (Bulgakov),
   11, 54*n*, 75*n*, 77*n*
Unitarianism, 38

V

Virgin Mary. *See* Mother of God

W

Western theology, 3, 5-7, 23
   Holy Spirit and, 45
   Russia ignored by, 11-12
   substance and, 25
Wisdom of God, 17-18
   angels and, 128
   Beast element rebelling
      against, 144-145
   biblical teaching and, 26-29
   Christ actualizing potentiality
      of, 94
   Church and, 134-136, 139
   compelling attraction of, 146-
      147
   creation of the world and, 67-
      71, 97
   freedom and, 148
   Glory and divine substance's
      relationship to, 31-36
   Holy Spirit and, 45, 46
   Holy Trinity and, 38-39
   human body analogous to

   Glory and, 58-59
   human nature and, 93
   live and vital thought as, 99
   Logos and, 43-45
   mariological interpretations of,
      124-128
   prototypes of creation and, 64-
      66, 69-70
   scholastic misunderstanding
      about, 54-55
   secularizing forces and, 20-21
   self-revelation of, 50
   sin and, 88
   tri-personal God and, 57
   unity of divine and the created,
      96
   Word anointed with Spirit and,
      101
Word of God, 86-87, 120, 136

155

ESALEN INSTITUTE / LINDISFARNE PRESS
LIBRARY OF RUSSIAN PHILOSOPHY

Though it only began to flourish in the nineteenth century, Russian philosophy has deep roots going back to the acceptance of Christianity by the Russian people in 988 and the subsequent translation into church Slavonic of the Greek Fathers. By the fourteenth century religious writings, such as those of Dionysius the Areopagite and Maximus the Confessor, were available in monasteries. Until the seventeenth century, then, except for some heterodox Jewish and Roman Catholic tendencies, Russian thinking tended to continue the ascetical, theological, and philosophical tradition of Byzantium, but with a Russian emphasis on the world's unity, wholeness, and transfiguration. It was as if a seed were germinating in darkness, for the centuries of Tartar domination and the isolationism of the Moscow state kept Russian thought apart from the onward movement of Western European thinking.

With Peter the Great (1672–1725), in Pushkin's phrase, a window was cut into Europe. This opened the way to Voltairian freethinking, while the striving to find ever greater depths in religious life continued. Freemasonry established itself in Russia, inaugurating a spiritual stream outside the church. Masons sought a deepening of the inner life, together with ideals of moral development and active love of one's neighbor. They drew on wisdom where they found it and were ecumenical in their sources. Thomas à Kempis's *Imitation of Christ* was translated, as were works by Saint-Martin ("The Unknown Philosopher"), Jacob Boehme, and the pietist Johann Arndt. Russian thinkers, too, became known by name: among others, Grigory Skovoroda (1722–1794), whose biblical interpretation drew upon Neoplatonism, Philo, and the German mystics; N.I. Novikov (1744–1818), who edited Masonic periodicals and organized libraries; the German I.G. Schwarz (1751–1784), a Rosicrucian follower of Jacob Boehme; and A.N. Radishchev (1749–1802), author of *On Man and His Immortality.*

There followed a period of enthusiasm for German idealism and, with the reaction to this by the Slavophiles Ivan Kireevksy and Alexei Khomyakov, independent philosophical thought in Russia was born. An important and still continuing tradition of creative thinking was initiated, giving rise to a whole galaxy of nineteenth and twentieth-century philosophers, including Pavel Yurkevitch, Nikolai Fedorov, Vladimir Solovyov, Leo Shestov, the Princes S. and E. Trubetskoy, Pavel Florensky, Sergius Bulgakov, Nikolai Berdyaev, Dmitri Merezhkovsky, Vassili Rozanov, Semon Frank, the personalists, the intuitionists, and many others.

Beginning in the 1840s, a vital tradition of philosophy entered the world stage, a tradition filled with as-yet unthought possibilities and implications not only for Russia herself but for the new multicultural, global reality humanity as a whole is now entering.

Characteristic features of this tradition are: *epistemological realism; integral knowledge* (knowledge as an organic, all-embracing unity that includes sensuous, intellectual, and mystical intuition); the celebration of *integral personality* (*tselnaya lichnost*), which is at once mystical, rational, and sensuous; and an emphasis upon the *resurrection* or *transformability* of the flesh. In a word, Russian philosophers sought a theory of the world as a whole, including its transformation.

Russian philosophy is simultaneously religious and psychological, ontological and cosmological. Filled with remarkably imaginative thinking about our global future, it joins speculative metaphysics, depth psychology, ethics, aesthetics, mysticism, and science with a profound appreciation of the world's movement toward a greater state. It is *bolshaya*, big, as philosophy should be. It is broad and individualistic, bearing within it many different perspectives—religious, metaphysical, erotic, social, and apocalyptic. Above all, it is universal. The principle of *sobornost* or all-togetherness (human catholicity) is of paramount importance in it. And it is future oriented, expressing a philosophy of history passing into *metahistory*, the life-of-the-world-to-come in the Kingdom of God.

At present, in both Russia and the West, there is a revival of interest in Russian philosophy, partly in response to the reductionisms implicit in materialism, atheism, analytic philosophy, deconstructionism, and so forth. On May 14, 1988, *Pravda* announced that it would publish the works of Solovyov, Trubetskoy, Semon Frank, Shestov, Florensky, Lossky, Bulgakov, Berdyaev, Alexsandr Bogdanov, Rozanov, and Fedorov. According to the announcement, thirty-five to forty volumes were to be published. This is now taking place.

The Esalen Institute–Lindisfarne Press Library of Russian Philosophy parallels this Russian effort. Since 1980 the Esalen Russian-American Exchange Center has worked to develop innovative approaches to Russian-American cooperation, sponsoring nongovernmental dialog and citizen exchange as a complement to governmental diplomacy. As part of its program, seminars are conducted on economic, political, moral, and religious philosophy. The Exchange Center aims to stimulate philosophic renewal in both the East and West. The Esalen-Lindisfarne Library of Russian Philosophy continues this process, expanding it to a broader American audience.

It is our feeling that these Russian thinkers—and those who even now are following in their footsteps—are world thinkers.

Publishing them will not only contribute to our understanding of the Russian people, but will also make a lasting contribution to the multicultural philosophical synthesis required by humanity around the globe as we enter the twenty-first century.